Dedication

To my children, Kevin, Cassie, and Kris, the first children I loved.
Tina Koch

To my parents, Fred and Jessie Ladewig, who gave me the gift of childhood.
Mary-Lane Kamberg

TIPS FROM TINA:

Help Around the House

Hundreds of Practical Ideas to Make Family Child Care Easier and More Fun

BY TINA KOCH AND MARY-LANE KAMBERG

Redleaf Press

a division of Resources for Child Caring

No part of this book is intended to conflict with existing child care laws or licensing regulations. The reader is responsible for compliance with laws and regulations governing child care and family child care licensing, as well as for ensuring the safety of the children in his or her care.

Cover and book design by MacLean & Tuminelly, Minneapolis, MN

Illustrations by Christina Tripp, Ontario, Canada

Published by: Redleaf Press
                 a division of Resources for Child Caring
                 450 N. Syndicate, Suite 5
                 St. Paul, MN 55104

Koch, Tina, 1943
     Tips from Tina: help around the house: hundreds of practical ideas to make
     family child care easier and more fun / by Tina Koch and Mary-Lane Kamberg.
          p.   cm.
     ISBN 1-884834-01-9
     1. Family day care—Activity programs—United States.
I. Kamberg, Mary-Lane, 1948- II. Title.
HV854.K63   1995
362.7 '12' 068—dc20

                                              95-10135   CIP

Acknowledgments

No idea becomes a published book without the help of people who contribute their ideas, talent, and encouragement during the writing and editing process. The authors would like to thank the following people for their help and support:

Kevin Koch, Cassie Koch Hansen, Kris Koch, Valerie Cable, Patricia Ireland, Joyce Kemnitz, Barbara Riley, Brock Ladewig, Kathy Dreiling, Edith Wells, Betsy Krusen, Linda Cordill, Andrea Warren, Candy Schock, Jane Berkowitz, Lois Daniel, Ken Kamberg, Becky Kamberg, Johanna Kamberg, members of the Kansas City Writers Group, librarians at the Johnson County Library and the Olathe Public Library, and our editors Eileen Nelson and Rosemary Wallner.

Contents

A Letter from Tina Koch

When the weather is cold I miss my years as a family child care provider more than at any other time. I imagine you sitting on your living room floor, reading stories while banana bread bakes for snacktime. Or are you out in the backyard, building a snowman with children who will never be cold enough to want to go inside?

I miss the days when I was one of you, juggling the jobs of mommy, book-keeper, chief cook (and bottle washer), nurse, and nanny. I cared for children of all ages in three different states as I raised my own three children. My job was filled with gummy smiles, peanut butter kisses, and more hugs than any Miss America could ever hope for. During those years, I searched for ways to simplify my day so I could spend more time with the children in my care. I also wanted to have some "me" left over at the end of the day. I read books and magazines, attended workshops, and networked with other child care providers. Bit by bit I found creative ways to save time, money, and effort.

Now I'd like to share these ideas with you. I wish we could sit down together so I could hear how you handle the challenges of family child care. I'd like to hear your ideas and tell you how I learned to organize my kitchen cup-boards, create storage space where none existed, and make mealtimes easier and more fun. This book is the next best thing.

In these pages you'll find hundreds of hints to make your child care life a little easier. Nothing will work for everyone every time, but I know you'll find ideas to try or adapt to your own use. Most of these tips are practical ways to get things done, but some ideas are just for fun. And that, after all, is what family child care is meant to be—these ideas gave me more time for fun. I hope they'll give you more time to laugh and snuggle with the children.

As I write to you today, a cold winter wind smells of new snow, the wet kind that's just right for packing into snowballs. My thoughts go out to you and the children in your care. When they wake up from their naps, please give them each a hug from me.

Tina Koch

Floor Plan:
How to Use this Book

The career you have chosen is a labor of love. But no matter how much you enjoy working with children, the routine tasks that go with the job of family child care provider can turn the best day to drudgery. This book is a collection of practical, hands-on tips designed to make your days easier and more fun.

This book resulted from hundreds of requests from family child care providers like you. They wanted an easy-to-use resource full of the tips Tina Koch used during her years as a family child care provider—the same ideas she presents in her provider training workshops and one-on-one consultations in providers' homes.

You'll find tips for every room in your home—and beyond. Each chapter contains tips for a specific room, with additional chapters for your basement, garage, and yard. You'll also find a chapter for the "Room in Your Heart." It has additional ways to show your love for the children in your care and parent communication suggestions.

Tips in chapter 3 are designed especially for family child care providers who participate in the Child and Adult Care Food Program (CACFP) sponsored by the U.S. Department of Agriculture. Along with ideas for food storage, the chapter has tips for easy ways to keep records, plan nutritious menus, organize shopping, and comply with CACFP policies and guidelines.

Where possible, the tips in this book are divided into subsections. For example, the "Helping Hands" subsections show you how to turn boring household tasks into fun activities for the children, who can help you with many of the jobs you usually do yourself. Children enjoy tasks you help make fun, especially when they know they're really helping. You'll lighten your workload and improve the children's self-confidence, self-esteem, and independence at the same time.

As you browse through the book's pages or look for an answer to a specific problem, you'll find easy ways to wash grungy highchairs, keep children from squabbling over where they sit at lunch, create storage space, and organize your child care business records even if you can't spare an extra room for a home office. And because your day is spent "giving, giving, giving" to the children in your care, as well as to your own family, each chapter also includes a "Just for You" tip, a way to do something nice for yourself or take a mini-break while the children are still there.

If you'd like ideas for materials you can use for art projects and other activities, check appendix A. You'll find a list of places in your community where you can get free or discounted items you can use for your child care.

Each chapter ends with room for your own ideas. Use this space to write in ideas from your experience or tips you get from other sources. As you record these ideas, you may think, "Other providers would love to try this!" If you'd like to share ways you make your family child care easier and more fun, fill out the form in appendix B and send it to us. Your idea might appear in a future book.

Finally, the tips in this book won't work for everyone every time. State regulations vary, and no one's home or particular situation is quite the same as anyone else's. As you read these suggestions, consider how they will work for you in your area. Use them as starting points for your own adaptations to help you bring less labor and more love to your family child care home.

Watch for this symbol!

Whenever a helpful tip is followed by

 IMPORTANT SAFETY TIP:

be sure to read and follow the safety tip. These are critically important tips that help you ensure the health and safety of the children in your care.

Chapter 1

Kitchen:

Is There Clutter in Your Butter?

Your kitchen is the hub of your family child care business, and no wonder. The work you do there dominates your day. You prepare meals and snacks and always seem to be cleaning something. The tips in this chapter are designed to take the drudgery out of kitchen chores and make your time in the kitchen a little easier. Your day will run more smoothly with colorful reminders and tips that shed light on dark corners. Your work will be done sooner, and you'll have more time for fun with the children in your care.

Soup Exchange

Plan a soup exchange with one or two friends who also have family child care businesses. Ask each provider to make a huge pot of a different kind of home-made soup. Divide the soup among the exchangers, with each provider keeping a portion of her own soup. Everyone gets a variety of soups to use for several lunches. Share recipes, too.

Ribbon Reminder

Tie a green ribbon to the refrigerator door handle to help you remember to administer medicine during the day and to remind you to send medication home with a child. Supplement the reminder with a small note, such as "Jordan's medicine 10 a.m./2 p.m." Use a kitchen magnet to fasten the note to the refrigerator door.

 IMPORTANT SAFETY TIP:

Be sure you comply with your state's regulations concerning written authorization from parents or physicians, as well as documentation of administering the medicine.

Ribbon Reminder II

If your state does not allow family child care providers to administer medications, use the ribbon reminder when you want to remember something else important. Or, use a different color ribbon for other reminders.

Baby's Drawer

Use one bottom kitchen drawer just for baby toys. Tie a pretty rattle to the handle. Teach the babies which drawer is theirs, and you won't have to say "no" as often.

Top Tip

Store all your lids for plastic containers in a plastic dishpan. Lids won't get lost, and you can pull out the dishpan and place it on the counter for easy selection of the right lid. The containers will take up less storage space because you can nestle them together.

Hot Potato

Bake potatoes in a muffin tin for easy going-in and coming-out of the oven.

Meat Loaf Muffins

Bake individual servings of meat loaf in muffin tins. If you have extra sections in the muffin tin, place small potatoes in them; the potatoes will be done at the same time.

Lunchtime

Children have a hard time understanding what you mean when you say, "We'll eat in a few minutes." Instead, set your kitchen timer to go off when your food is almost ready. Tell the children that when they hear the timer, it will be time to wash their hands and come to the table.

Winter Blah Breaker

Plan a Hawaiian luau lunch to beat the winter blahs. Give children individual lunch bags to draw on while you fix food to take to the "beach." Fill the lunch bags, then spread beach towels on the table. Play Hawaiian music and let the children wear sunglasses and leis while they eat.

Quick Fix

Make your life easier by cooking twice as much dinner as you need for your family. Use the planned leftovers for child care lunch the next day. It will be ready in five minutes with the help of your microwave.

Daily Grind

If you have a meat grinder or can borrow one, buy several chuck roasts and a box of Ziploc resealable freezer bags. Trim the roasts and grind your own hamburger while the children watch. They'll be fascinated, and you'll all eat healthier, low-fat ground beef. Divide into quantities you use regularly, and freeze for future recipes.

Syrup Substitute

If you're out of syrup on a pancake morning, open a can of frozen apple juice. Do not dilute. Heat and use as syrup for a yummy, natural substitute.

Reheat Treat

Reheated pizza crust goes limp in the microwave, so use your electric griddle instead. Place the cold pizza on a lightly greased or nonstick surface griddle pre-heated to 300 degrees. Make a tent over it with a long sheet of aluminum foil. Crimp the edges of the foil, being careful not to let the tent touch the pizza's cheese topping. Heat until the cheese is soft and the bottom is crispy.

That's (NOT) Italian!

If Italian salad dressing on pasta salad is too tangy for the children, substitute creamy ranch dressing. They'll ask for seconds.

Breakaway Tacos

Children love tacos, but the shells break and make a mess. Instead, serve taco salad. Break the corn tortillas into small pieces. Place the tortilla pieces in a bowl and top with the rest of the ingredients. Let children eat it with a spoon.

 IMPORTANT SAFETY TIP:

Be sure tortilla pieces are small enough to avoid a choking hazard.

No Strings Attached

Use your potato peeler to remove "strings" from celery ribs for peanut butter and celery snacks for children who are three years old and up. The children won't complain about strings getting caught between their teeth.

 IMPORTANT SAFETY TIP:

Don't serve celery to children younger than three years of age; it can be a choking hazard.

Sunny Side Up

Use tuna can rings to keep eggs from running together on a griddle.

Quick Snips

Use kitchen scissors (a pair you use only for food preparation) to cut pizza, sandwiches, raw bacon, chicken, and stew beef. The scissors work much faster than knives.

Dicey Dogs

For an easy, imaginative main dish, cut two hot dogs lengthwise, then dice. Add to a can of baked beans or a bowl of macaroni and cheese.

 IMPORTANT SAFETY TIP:

Hot dogs can be a choking hazard; be sure pieces are small enough so they do not get caught in a child's throat.

Rings Around the Griddle

Save twelve tuna cans and remove the tops and bottoms, leaving only the rings. Spray the insides with cooking spray and arrange the rings on a long, nonstick electric griddle. You can now make a dozen perfectly round pancakes by pouring the batter into the center of the rings.

 IMPORTANT SAFETY TIPS:

Be careful to avoid any sharp edges. Use tongs to remove the rings when you're ready to flip the pancakes.

Pineapple Wheels

Use tuna can rings to make a fun fruit and gelatin salad. Set the rings on a large, flat pan and place a pineapple slice in the bottom of each. Pour your favorite flavor of gelatin dessert over the pineapple and chill until set. Twist and wiggle the ring and use a spatula to ease out the pineapple wheel.

Round and Crispy

Use tuna can rings to form round Rice Krispie cereal treats.

For Veggie Haters Only

If you have children who refuse to eat vegetables, try this. In a blender, combine chunks of raw celery and carrots with 1 1/2 cups of water. In a few seconds, you'll have finely chopped pieces. Pour the mixture through a strainer, pushing out excess water with the back of a spoon. Add the mixture to stews, soups, burgers, or cooked potatoes you plan to mash. You'll meet the children's nutritional requirements, and they'll never know how good you've been to them.

 IMPORTANT SAFETY TIP:

Be sure vegetable pieces are small enough to avoid a choking hazard.

Pizza Cutters

Use tuna can rings to cut individual pizza crusts.

Helping Hands

The more child care work you do during the day, the more time and energy you'll have for yourself and your family at night. One way to have more time is to plan and prepare meals while your children are there. When children help prepare food, their likelihood of eating it increases. Try the following ideas to turn kitchen chores into enjoyable activities.

Delicious Devils

Making deviled eggs is easy with help from the children. Arrange hard-boiled egg white halves on a serving plate and put the yolks in a Ziploc resealable bag. Add mayonnaise, mustard, sweet pickle relish, or whatever other ingredients you prefer to the bag, then seal it. Let children take turns rolling and mashing the ingredients together with a rolling pin. When thoroughly mixed, cut off one of the corners of the bag. Squeeze the mixture into the waiting egg whites and top with paprika or parsley. Just throw away the bag—no mess and no mixing bowl to wash. (Add a glass of fruit juice or milk for a complete snack.)

Nutty Nana Roll-Ups

Follow the directions for Delicious Devils, but arrange slices of bread on a serving plate instead of the egg halves. Place three heaping tablespoons of peanut butter and two very ripe bananas into the Ziploc resealable bag. Have the children gently roll and mash the ingredients with a rolling pin. Then cut off one of the corners of the bag and squeeze the mixture onto the bread. Roll the bread for a nutty snack.

Cookie Art

Children love to decorate holiday and party cookies, but if you don't have time to bake, use graham crackers instead. The children will be just as happy to decorate the crackers.

Cookie Art II

If children can't manipulate your frosting tool to decorate cookies, muffins, or graham crackers, give each child some frosting in a small Ziploc resealable bag. Cut 1/4 inch off the corner of the bag and let the child squeeze the bag to create an edible work of art. Throw away used bags for easy cleanup.

It's in the Bag

Mix meat loaf using a Ziploc resealable bag. Put all the ingredients into the bag and have the children take turns squeezing until everything is thoroughly mixed.

Chef for a Day

If letting all the children help at mealtime seems too hectic, let one child be Helper of the Day. Use a smiley face button or make a Helper of the Day badge out of construction paper. Or, for a fun prop, buy a real chef's hat from a restaurant supplier. Use your kitchen calendar to rotate assignments so everyone gets a turn.

Spoon Masters

To make it easier for a child to help you stir, place a damp dishcloth under the bowl to keep it from sliding.

Searchlight

Keep a flashlight in your kitchen drawer. When you can't see under the sink or in the back of your cupboards because it's too dark, ask one of the children to hold the flashlight for you while you search.

Toy Bath

While you supervise, let the children give washable toys a bath in the kitchen sink. If you have a double sink, run about 4 inches of warm, soapy water in each side. Let two children at a time stand on chairs while you watch them scrub toys with old toothbrushes. (Adapt to one at a time if you have a single sink.) Set the timer for five-minute turns. Rinse toys and air dry in the dish drainer or on beach towels. Or, let children who are waiting for their turns dry the toys. This activity does not replace the disinfecting you give the toys as regulated by your state.

 IMPORTANT SAFETY TIP:

Never leave children unattended around any water source.

Keeping the Mess Out of Your Mess Hall

You have enough to do without spending your whole day cleaning the kitchen! These tips will help you avoid drips, spots, and spatters before they have a chance to settle onto your walls, floors, and furniture. You'll stop spills before they happen, and clean up those inevitable accidents quickly. Spend a few minutes setting up these prevention inventions.

"Extra" Clean

Is your refrigerator so close to the stovetop that grease spatters on it when you fry food? Before cooking, use kitchen magnets to secure a sheet of aluminum foil to the side of the refrigerator. Just throw the foil, and the spatters, away when you finish cooking.

Cool, Clean Crisper

Line your refrigerator crisper drawer with an old cloth place mat. It fits easily, and when it gets dirty, simply put in a fresh one and wash the dirty one.

Easy Hang-Ups

Keep your kitchen telephone clean and easy to grip with wet or sticky hands by cutting off the cuff of an old crew sock. Slip it over the handset. If you have a touch-tone telephone with buttons in the handset, simply slide the cover up or down to dial. The cover is easy to replace or remove for washing.

 IMPORTANT SAFETY TIP:

Long telephone cords can pose a strangulation hazard. Be sure to wind up and bind excess cord and hang out of children's reach.

Stick No More

When a cookie recipe tells you to roll cookie dough into a ball, use cooking spray on the palms of your hands first. The dough won't cling to your fingers.

Clearly Clean

Use clear plastic wrap to cover blender buttons. The wrap catches the spatters, and you can still see the buttons. Throw the wrap away when you're finished.

Dish Drainer Puddle Preventer

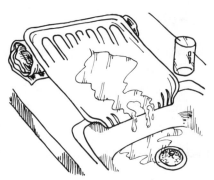

Keep water from forming a puddle on the rubber mat under your dish drainer. Before doing dishes, place a rolled-up newspaper under the mat at the end away from the sink. You'll create an incline, and water will drain into the sink.

Easy Cleanups

Even the best ounce-of-prevention tactics don't eliminate the need to clean the kitchen. But that doesn't mean you have to spend the whole day doing it. Get the grit out of the nitty gritty. These easy tips will help you clean your counters, small appliances, and even the children! Your kitchen will sparkle, and you'll have more time at the end of the day.

On-the-Spot Spot Remover

Remove stubborn food coloring or drink powder stains from your counter top with this on-the-spot spot remover. Use a medicine bottle with an eyedropper stopper. Fill it with a mixture of chlorine bleach and water in the ratio of one tablespoon bleach per quart of water. Test a small, unnoticeable area of the surface to be sure chlorine bleach will not harm it. Apply one drop of the mixture to the stain. Wait sixty seconds and sponge off.

 IMPORTANT SAFETY TIPS:

Store out of children's reach. Use masking tape and a marker to clearly label the bottle's contents.

Drip Stoppers

Wrist bands cut from old crew sock cuffs keep your arms free from drips when you wash windows or do other "drippy" chores.

Dish Drainer Soak

At bedtime empty your dish drainer and place it and its mat in the sink. Fill the sink with very hot water, 1/4 cup of laundry detergent, and 1/2 cup of chlorine bleach. Soak overnight. In the morning use a bottle brush to get grime out of cracks and crevices. Rinse, and your drainer will be sanitized and good as new.

Chair Rub Down

Clean chair sides and backs with old cotton socks. Slip the socks on your hands and dip into sudsy dishwater. Wring out, then rub up and down the chairs. Clean after meals and snacks before anything sticky has a chance to harden. Children love to help with this job, so have extra socks on hand for them.

Pipe Cleaner Cleanup

Use a fuzzy pipe cleaner to clean the blade of your electric can opener. Unplug the opener. Dip the pipe cleaner in hot soapy water and run it around the can opener blade. (You may need more than one pipe cleaner.) When you're finished, use a dry pipe cleaner to dry the blade.

 IMPORTANT SAFETY TIP:

Be sure the can opener is unplugged before attempting to clean it.

Pipe Cleaner Cleanup II

Use a fuzzy pipe cleaner to clean around the base of grungy faucets.

Sparkling Stove Tops

Soak stove-top grills and drip pans overnight in a sink full of hot water and 1/4 cup of laundry detergent.

Dishwasher Delights

Your dishwasher will wash more than dishes. Use it for baby bottle nipples, toys, stove-top drip pans, and even the kitchen sponge. Try these tips for easy, no-scrub cleanups.

Berry Clean Baby Bottle Nipples

Two plastic berry baskets and two twist ties make a convenient container for washing baby bottle nipples in the dishwasher. Place the nipples in one basket. Invert the other for the top. Secure with twist ties. Place the container on the top rack of the dishwasher. This is a "berry" good idea for all small, washable items.

No-Scrub Stove Tops

Whenever you run a load of dishes, add your stove-top grills and drip pans to the bottom rack of your dishwasher to eliminate scouring sessions.

Sweet Scrubbers

To keep your dishcloth, sponge, and plastic scrubbers fresh, toss them on the top rack of the dishwasher and run them with a load of dishes.

Freezer Bag Recycling

Recycle Ziploc freezer bags by washing them with liquid dish detergent. Rinse and turn them upside down to drip dry on the bottom rack of your empty dishwasher.

 IMPORTANT SAFETY TIP:

Remove bags before running dishwasher.

Toy Wash

You can wash teething toys in the top rack of the dishwasher. Cut a piece of nylon net large enough to nestle into the top rack. Place toys on top of the netting and they won't fall through.

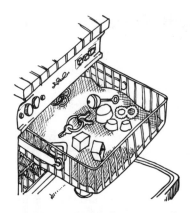

Safety First

After you've carefully stored poisons, medicines, and household cleaners and taken all the safety steps required by your state's regulatory agency, you can still make your family child care home safer. Use the back burners of your stove instead of the front ones whenever you can. Be sure to turn pot handles toward the back of the stove to make it difficult for children to reach them. Lock away knives and other dangerous utensils. Keep plastic bags and boxes of plastic wraps out of children's reach. Unplug small appliances when not in use and wind up and bind excess cord. In addition to these tips, the following ideas will help you avoid burns and falls and handle minor emergencies.

No Exit

Install swinging cafe doors at floor level instead of a baby gate. Put a latch on the outside, down low, where you can reach over to unlatch it, but a child cannot. Buy the kind of doors that can be opened all the way back to the walls so you can keep them in the open position when you are not doing child care. These doors also keep pets out of the kitchen.

Frozen First Aid

A bag of frozen peas or corn makes a quick ice pack for injuries. When a child gets a bump or sprain, simply hit the bag on a counter or other surface to loosen the vegetables, then apply to the "boo-boo" to keep down swelling. Be sure to place a dry dishcloth or kitchen towel under the bag to protect the child's skin.

Red Flag First Aid

Place a clean, dry red washcloth in a plastic bag and keep it in a kitchen drawer. When a child gets a bloody wound, dampen the cloth with cool water, wring out, and apply. The blood won't show up against the red cloth, so the child won't be as frightened.

Red Means Stop

Help children know when your stove is hot by tying a red bow on the oven door when the oven or stove top is in use. Tell the children, "Red means stop."

Just for You

R and R

Use a yellow place mat when you need a "good" time out in the kitchen. Tell the children that when you're using your yellow place mat, the only way they can sit with you is to bring a quiet activity to the table. Set the kitchen timer for five minutes. Then sit at the table with a cup of coffee or other refreshment. Put up your feet and relax.

Your Own Ideas

Use this space to write your own kitchen ideas and tips. To find out how to share your ideas, see appendix B.

_____

_____

_____

_____

_____

_____

Chapter 2

Dining Room:
At Your (Food) Service

Y ou and the children in your care will have fun with food using these hints for serving meals and snacks. Everyone needs a break from routine, and you'll provide variety and entertainment with fun ways to slurp cereal milk and decide who sits where at lunch. Some of these ideas simply serve to avoid conflicts, others offer new ideas for setting the table and serving food. Bon appétit!

Family Style

Always sit and eat with the children. Model good eating habits and manners. Encourage playful conversation and a relaxed attitude. Meals are more enjoyable when there's a sense of family togetherness.

I'd Like to Introduce...

When introducing a new food, use hors d'oeuvre forks (found in the party section at your grocery store). Serve the new food cut in small pieces. As an incentive to sample it, use the forks only for the new food.

New Food on the Block

To introduce an unfamiliar food, serve it to yourself, but don't offer it to the children. When they ask why they don't have any, say, "It's 'Big People Food.' I'm not sure you're old enough to try it." Tell them you'll think about it. On the next day, tell them that maybe you'll fix them some tomorrow. By the third day, the children will be eager to try the new food.

Eat Like a Bird

When you have several boxes of cereal with just a little in each one, combine them all in a plastic bag. Add a handful of raisins and a handful of sunflower seed kernels. Shake to mix. Serve in small paper cups and call it "Kiddie Birdseed." For extra fun, take the snack outside, sit in the grass, and enjoy with a cup of fruit juice.

This Side Up

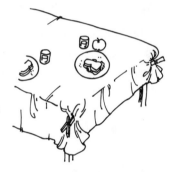

At mealtime use a flannel-backed tablecloth with the flannel side up. The flannel absorbs spilled liquids and keeps dishes from slipping. It feels better on little elbows, too. Keep the tablecloth in place by securing the corners with spring-type clothespins.

Sweetheart Place Cards

Avoid conflicts over who sits where at mealtime with heart-shaped place cards. Cut out red poster board hearts the size of your palm. Label a heart for each child. Just before sitting down, shuffle the hearts and deal them out face down around the table. Turn them over to show where each "sweetheart" will sit.

Feeling Their Oats

Cool and flavor hot oatmeal with ice cubes made of frozen apple juice. Drop one apple juice ice cube in the center of each bowl of oatmeal. Tell children to stir until the ice cube melts.

Drinks All Day

In hot weather label an insulated plastic sport bottle (the kind with a big plastic straw sticking out) for each child. Fill with ice cubes and cold water in the morning and keep on a low table or shelf so children can help themselves. You'll eliminate frequent openings of the refrigerator.

 IMPORTANT SAFETY TIP:

If you use these bottles outside, avoid sweet drinks or bees may swarm.

Easy Centerpiece

Use a nonpoisonous or silk potted plant for an attractive centerpiece.

Center of Attention

Bring beauty, joy, and conversation to your table by using a simple seasonal centerpiece each day. Use spring dandelions, summer melons, autumn leaves, or a winter holiday decoration such as an empty valentine candy box. During meals, stimulate conversation by asking questions like: How many dandelions are in our bowl today? Where do melons grow? How many colors of leaves are there? Who is your sweetheart?

Moo Down

Cut drinking straws in half and let children use them to drink the leftover milk out of cereal bowls. Even reluctant milk drinkers can't resist a straw.

Easy Upholstery Cover-Ups

Protect upholstered kitchen or dining room chairs by covering the seats and backs with bath towels. Sew Velcro fastening tape on opposite ends of the towel. The towel attaches to itself for easy-on/easy-off use. Toss in the washing machine every few days.

Summer Snow Cones

Buy a bag of shaved ice and place the ice in paper cups. Add thawed, undiluted orange-pineapple juice to make your own snow cones. Use other juice flavors for variety. Add graham crackers for a complete snack.

Please Pass the Ketchup

Serve ketchup, tartar sauce, vegetable dips, etc., in paper baking cups. The children have fun, and cleanup is a breeze. Just throw away the cups.

Instant Booster Chair

If your dining room or kitchen chairs are stackable, use two stacked chairs instead of a booster chair to help a toddler get high enough to reach the table.

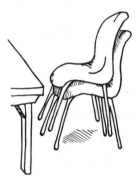

Table Talk

A redwood picnic table with separate benches economizes space in your dining area. Between meals you can push the table against the wall, with benches stored underneath. Let children use carpet squares under their knees if they have to kneel on the benches to reach the table. (Carpet square samples are available in a variety of sizes from carpet stores; see appendix A.) Children can also use the benches for other activities like making a clubhouse, setting up an obstacle course, or playing choo-choo train.

Table Knife Substitutes

Table knives are too big and heavy for most children. Instead, give them butter knives or cheese spreaders when they are learning to apply their own butter, mayonnaise, or other spreadables. (Ask friends and family to save extra cheese knives from holiday food trays.)

 IMPORTANT SAFETY TIP:

Avoid plastic knives with serrated edges. Children may drag them across their tongues and cut themselves.

Drip Stoppers

Wrist bands cut from crew sock cuffs stop drips from watermelon or melting juice pops that run down a child's arm.

Nonskid Kids

Apply bathtub nonskid decals to your highchair seat to keep the baby from sliding off.

 IMPORTANT SAFETY TIP:

Always be sure to use highchair safety straps as well.

Yipes! Wipes!

Keep a container of moist pop-up wipes in the dining area. Clean children's hands and faces after eating. You'll have fewer fingerprints to clean off walls, toys, and furniture.

Handy Hand Towel

Attach a magnetic towel bar to the back of your highchair. Hang a clean, damp hand towel or washcloth there for meals and snacks. The towel is handy for quick cleanups before getting the child down. You can also hang the bib on the towel bar.

 IMPORTANT SAFETY TIP:

Always supervise a child in a highchair and be sure to use safety straps.

Bandanna Bibs

Use colorful 100 percent cotton bandanna handkerchiefs for inexpensive bibs
the children will enjoy. Fold on the bias
and sew Velcro fastening tape on diagonal
corners for easy attachment and removal.
The bandanna bibs are absorbent and
easy to launder. Be sure to have plenty on
hand, because older children will use
them to play cowboys.

Color of the Day

Buy colorful plastic picnic plates and glasses and assign each child a color of the
day. For example, Jonathan uses the green plate and cup, Joanne uses red, and
Megan gets yellow. Keep track of who has which color by using that color to
spell out the children's names on the refrigerator using magnetic plastic letters
from toy letter boards. Or, make a chart with each child's name and place it on
your refrigerator. Place magnetic colored squares beside each name. Rotate the
colors each day.

No Tears Over Spilled Milk

Put a pad of newspaper under toddlers' lunch plates to help identify their
places. Personalize the newspaper place mat by writing the child's name on it
with a red marking pen. Then add a smiley face circle at the top to indicate
placement of the glass or cup, out of the "spill range." The newsprint will absorb
messes and soak up spilled milk before it can run onto the floor.

Spill Stoppers

Covered plastic cups with drinking spouts are
great for babies, but older children may balk
at using them. Cut off half the spout and slip
a drinking straw through the opening to make
the cups special for older children.

Helping Hands

Get the children into the act when it's time to set the table and serve meals and snacks. They'll feel responsible and independent as they contribute. Remind them to wash their hands before helping with these activities.

Get Ready!

Reserve a low cupboard or shelf for the child-sized dishes, utensils, and cups you use for child care. Let the children get out the tableware and set the table.

Get Set!

The children can help you set the table if you help them remember where everything goes. Buy a plastic tablecloth and a permanent marker. Draw the place settings where you want them by tracing the plates, cups, forks, spoons, and napkins. The patterns are easy for children to follow and help them remember to keep their glasses "on the circles," instead of at the edge of the table.

Get Set! II

Let children help set the table by giving each one an assignment (Lindsey: glasses; Shay: plates). Set the items they'll need where they can reach them. Have the children take turns doing their jobs one at a time so they don't run into each other.

Place Mat Art

To keep the children from getting restless while you cook, have them create their own place mats while they wait. Provide pens, markers, and paper (you can get free paper from real estate agents who change multiple listing binders monthly; see appendix A for other sources of paper). Keep everything in a special container to be used only for place mat art. When the food is ready, serve it on their place mats.

Name that Food

Children love a sense of fun, so use zany names for the foods you serve. Milk can be "Moo Juice." Peas can be "Monkey's Marbles." Let the children help you create the names.

Just for You

At Your (Postal) Service

Save your junk mail or ask parents to bring you theirs. Bring it to the table along with gummed stamps from contests or magazine subscription offers. Let the children play post office while you write a letter to a friend.

Your Own Ideas

Use this space to write your own food serving ideas. To find out how to share your ideas, see appendix B.

_____

_____

_____

_____

_____

_____

_____

_____

_____

_____

_____

Tips from Tina

Chapter 3

Pantry:
CACFP and
Menu Mania

Use these ideas to plan menus and keep your child care food from taking over your kitchen. These tips will help you save time and money and suggest ways to organize your refrigerator, freezer, and cupboards.

Many of the tips in this chapter are designed for family child care providers who participate in the U.S. Department of Agriculture's Child and Adult Care Food Program (CACFP). CACFP is a federal nutrition education program that reimburses child care providers for serving foods that comply with the program's pattern for good nutrition. Providers furnish menus that show the foods they served, and CACFP issues a monthly reimbursement. Local sponsors administer CACFP, and their systems may differ from state to state. Adapt these ideas to conform to procedures used by the sponsoring agency in your area. If you're not on CACFP and are interested in participating, find a program sponsor in your phone book and call for information.

It's in the Cards

This easy system for menu planning and grocery shopping takes time to set up, but once it's in place, it will make your job less hectic. You'll need a file box, colored markers, and 3-by-5-inch index cards.

On one side of each card, print a different menu for a breakfast, a lunch, or a snack. If the meal or snack contains vitamin C, draw an orange star on the top of the card. Draw a red star for iron and a green one for vitamin A. Some menu cards will have more than one star on them. On the back of each card, list the ingredients needed for that meal.

On Friday, select meal and snack cards from your file box for the coming week. Turn the cards over and make your shopping list. Then file the cards behind tabs for each day, Monday through Friday. You'll be prepared for the whole week. You can also use the back of the file box to store recipes. Start with three week's worth of cards. Continue adding new menu cards so the children get a variety of new foods.

Menu Highlights

Use colored highlighting markers on your weekly menu to mark the foods that contain iron and vitamins A and C. This system will help ensure that you meet the children's nutrition requirements so you qualify for reimbursement for meals you serve.

Easy Menus

Let your local school system's food service director plan your child care meals. Simply follow the school lunch menu. The guidelines school systems follow will comply with your nutrition needs for CACFP for all children, except infants. Some school district dietitians plan menus as much as a year in advance. Ask if they are willing to share them with you (many will be happy to do so). If not, local newspapers often publish school menus. Look for them there, or get a copy from your own children, older siblings of the children in your care, or a neighbor with children in school.

Menu Planners

Have the children take turns helping you plan the week's menu. Each child chooses a day's menu and helps in the kitchen that day. Use this opportunity to teach the food pyramid by offering several choices for each item and letting the "chef" select from your suggestions. To order a copy of "The Food Guide Pyramid" booklet, send a $1.00 check or money order made out to the Superintendent of Documents to: Consumer Information Center, Department 119-A, Pueblo, Colorado 81009.

Put Togethers

To avoid throwing out leftovers on Saturday, go through the refrigerator on Thursday night to see what you can combine for Friday's lunch or snacks. A few peach slices and pineapple chunks will make a fruit salad if you slice in a couple of bananas. Two hot dogs can be sliced lengthwise then diced and added to macaroni and cheese or to a can of beans for a main dish. Use your imagination, and you'll surprise yourself and the children.

 IMPORTANT SAFETY TIP:

Hot dogs can be a choking hazard; be sure pieces are small enough so they do not get caught in a child's throat.

Friday Fun

On Fridays you're likely to have two chicken legs, one hot dog, two pear halves, a cup of fruit cocktail, two bananas, small amounts of two or three vegetables, and parts of bags of rolls and loaves of bread left from the week's meals. Prepare and place all the leftovers on the kitchen counter and draw names to let the children take turns selecting items from all the food groups in the food pyramid. Children love this lunch buffet! (For CACFP members, write "meat/fruit-veg-etable/bread/milk" on your menu. At the bottom of the menu, note the items each child took.)

Copy Cat

Make copies of your menus before sending them to your CACFP sponsor. You'll be glad you did if they ever get lost in the mail or if you are audited.

Picture Perfect

Let the children help you plan menus. Cut out pictures of foods from magazines. Place empty plates on the table and let children choose an item from each food pyramid group that they would like for a meal. Write their ideas on a menu. Monday can be Mandy's day. Tuesday can be Allison's day, and so on.

Hang it Up

Parents like to know what foods their children are being served. Use heavy-duty magnetic clips to secure your menu pads on the refrigerator door for parents to read. Make photocopies each week to send home.

Snacks in Shifts

If you serve snacks in shifts because some children go home before schoolagers arrive, your CACFP menu pages may look like you're over-enrolled. Draw a star next to the names of children who leave early. At the bottom of each menu page, note the time they leave and the time the schoolagers arrive.

Paper Saver

Laminate a blank menu page and use a grease pencil or wipe-off marker to plan your week's menu. When you've served the meals and recorded your daily attendance, copy it onto your CACFP sponsor's menu form. Wipe the laminated menu clean, and it's ready for the next week's planning.

Menus by Mail

If you mail your menus to your CACFP sponsor, save time by pre-addressing your envelopes. Get twelve large envelopes (one for each month) and write your sponsor's address and your return address on each. Stamp them and put them in a file. As you get enrollment forms, place them into the front envelope. When it's time to send in your menus for the month, your enrollment forms will already be inside. Add the menus, seal, and mail.

"Never Late" Date

Predate menu sheets from your CACFP sponsor. In the column under the date you are to mail in your menus, write "SEND." On your calendar, write "SEND" to remind you to send in your menus.

Your Number's Up

Some CACFP sponsors provide a list of numbered menu choices that satisfy nutrition guidelines. (For example, menu choice #2002 is grilled cheese, tomato soup, peaches, bread, and milk.) If your CACFP sponsor supplies numbered menus, get your copies laminated and tack them to the inside of your cupboard door. They'll always be handy when you need to plan meals.

Stick 'em Up

Hang a calendar above your desk and place smiley face stickers on the squares for the days you are to mail in your menus to your food program sponsor. Do all twelve months and be ready for the year.

Whether the Weather

If you live where snow and ice can keep you from getting out in winter, be sure to keep extra milk, juice, and bread in the freezer. Stock shelves with extra pasta, rice, peanut butter, and canned meats, fruits, and vegetables. You can always put meals together if you don't run out of staples.

Master List

Type a master list of grocery items, arranged in categories. Put a short line in front of each item where you can write quantities. Make photocopies of the list and file the original for later reuse. Post a blank list on the refrigerator each week and mark items as you run out of them. Add to the list when you plan your menu for the coming week.

Follow the Plan

If your grocery store provides a map of its floor plan that locates items by aisle, use it to determine the order of your master grocery list. You'll save shopping time by not having to double back for forgotten items.

Clip-On Coupons

Keep your grocery list on a clipboard while you shop. Put your coupons under the clip as you select those items. Keep a pencil under the clip to cross off each item on the list as you place it in your grocery cart.

Night Stocker

Grocery shopping can be hectic with children along, so why not shop at night? Let your spouse or a friend stay home with your own children so you can shop alone. The store will be nearly empty, and you'll finish in half the time it takes during the day. If you go the night before the grocery ads come out, shelves will be fully stocked, and sale prices may already be in the store's computer system. Ask your store manager.

Money Matters

Any business will realize bigger profits when economical measures are in place. Watch for store specials, double or triple coupon discounts, or two-for-one offers. In addition, use these tips to keep child care costs down without cutting corners.

Envelopes on File

Use a handy envelope system to be sure you don't lose those all-important receipts for child care food. Write your grocery list on the outside of an envelope and put the date on the top corner. Put your coupons inside and go shopping. Write your check number or the word "cash" on the grocery receipt tape while you are still in the store. Then put the tape into the envelope. Keep the same envelope in your purse all week to keep all of that week's receipts. At the end of the week, file the envelope and replace it with a new one.

Coupon Savers

Ask your child care parents to bring in coupons they don't use. Preschoolers can help you cut them out and sort them. You'll save time and money, and preschoolers will get good cutting practice.

Coupon Savers II

Start a coupon "swap box" with your neighbors. Take coupons for items you use and replace them with coupons for items you don't. You'll all save money.

Coupon Savers III

Ask four year olds (who always love to cut) to clip your Sunday coupons. They can sit at the kitchen table and work while you fix lunch. When they finish, take out the ones you use and let them play store with the others.

Paper or Plastic?

Buy canvas "earth bags" to use on grocery shopping trips instead of paper or plastic bags. They hold up to 60 pounds and never rip out while being carried into the house. They're washable, too. Best of all, they're better for the environment and can save you money. Many stores allow credit for each earth bag you use.

Make a Wish

Serve muffins instead of cupcakes for children's birthdays. Cupcakes have too much sugar, so they don't qualify for reimbursement on CACFP. However, muffins do. Serve with milk or juice. The children won't notice the difference.

Folder Holder

Buy a colorful binder and a three-hole punch to use for correspondence from your CACFP sponsor. File items by date, and circle training sessions and workshops on your calendar. When you earn a training certificate, put this in the binder, too. When it's time to renew your license, you'll have proof of training hours at your fingertips.

Sweeten the Deal

Sweet cereals don't qualify as reimbursable foods on CACFP, but children want them. Buy one box of sugared cereal and use some to fill an empty sugar bowl. When you serve healthy cereal, let the children take one spoonful of sugared cereal to sprinkle on top in place of a spoonful of sugar.

Pick a Peck

If there's an orchard or "picking field" in your area, take the children on an outing to pick apples, berries, or other produce. You'll have a great time and get fresh food at bargain prices. Ask the orchard or field manager how best to store the food.

Make it Yourself

If you have a baby in care who is eating fruits and vegetables, you can make your own baby food from many of the fruits and vegetables you feed older children. First, rinse foods that may be too salty or too sweet. Then place them in a blender or food processor and puree.

Make it Yourself II

Ask at your library or bookstore for a "make a mix" cookbook that has recipes for pancake, cookie, and muffin mixes. A number of these cookbooks are on the market. Look through several and buy the one you like best. You'll save time and money making your own mixes.

Check it Out

Open a separate checking account for your child care business. When you write a check for child care food, write "CACFP" on the memo line. You'll track your spending patterns and easily identify child care expenses.

Buy in Bulk

If your CACFP sponsor offers bulk food purchasing, take advantage of the savings. If you have limited storage space, you can still save by splitting cases with another family child care provider.

Members Only

Join a wholesale food club and save. Memberships often accommodate two families, so share the membership with another provider. If you must drive a long distance to enjoy club benefits, try to form a group of three or four providers who can go to the club together once a month. Have lunch out and enjoy yourselves.

Join the Club

Try starting a bulk food purchase cooperative in your area if one is not available. Call the head cook of your nearest elementary school or your school district's director of food services to find out who they buy from. Go from there. Be sure everyone who participates pays in advance so you don't get stuck with extra expense and unwanted food.

Food Stocks

You can have money left over from your December CACFP check if you stock up on canned goods, frozen juices, and other nonperishables between August and November. Buy plenty when they're on sale, and you'll have a stockpile of groceries. In December you'll need to buy only fresh food, leaving additional money for holiday extras.

Grain Group

Scout around for a bakery outlet that sells overstocked products, rather than old stock. You'll save between 30 and 50 percent on bread and rolls.

Food Storage

The best food planning won't work if you can't find a certain item when you need it. Use these ideas to make storing food easier. Your shelves will stay neat, and you'll save food preparation time.

Ice Box Box

Before freezing a loaf of bread, slip it inside an empty saltine cracker box. This helps the bread keep its shape.

Freezer Flats

Use Ziploc freezer bags to freeze foods such as soup, chili, and spaghetti sauce. Fill the bag and lay it flat in the freezer. Food stored this way takes up less room than food stored in plastic containers, and it takes less time to defrost.

Mother Hubbard's Cupboard

Reserve one cupboard or shelf for child care food storage. When you unpack your groceries for the week's menu, arrange the food in the order it will be used, with Monday's items in front.

Spice Up Your Shelves

Use a clear plastic shoe box to store spice tins and bottles. Place a layer of spice containers face down in the bottom of the box. Then place another layer face up. When you need a spice, look through the clear lid to find the one you want. Can't find it? Lift the box and read labels through the clear plastic bottom.

Off Limits

To keep your child care food separate from your family's food, place a rubber band around the box, can, or jar when you unpack your child care groceries. Use a particular bowl to store child care fruit in the refrigerator. Tell your family these items are off limits.

Clothespin Closers

Use spring-type clothespins to reclose cereal pouches and freezer bags. Clothespins also work well to keep cookbooks open to your place.

Baby Bottle Storage

Keep baby bottles in a cardboard soft drink six-pack carton to keep them from falling over in the refrigerator.

Sticky Stuff

Keep syrup and honey bottles from leaving sticky spots on your cupboard shelves. Attach a paper coffee filter to the bottom of the bottle with a rubber band. The filter will absorb sticky drips, so your shelves will stay clean.

Sticky Stuff II

Make a drip guard for bottles that contain sticky stuff. Cut off the top of an old crew sock and slip the cuff onto the bottle to absorb drips that run down the side.

Top it Off

Tubs from margarine and whipped topping are great for storing leftovers, but you can't see what's inside. Put a self-sticking label on the lid and identify the contents with a marker. Write small so you can cross out the item and use the same label for the next leftover. When you fill up the label, put a new one on top.

Just for You

Dining Out

Use coupons when you buy child care food. After shopping, put the amount you saved in a canister on a pantry shelf. At the end of the month, empty your savings and go out to eat. Let someone wait on you!

Your Own Ideas

Use this space to write your own food storage and shopping ideas. To find out how to share your ideas, see appendix B.

_____

_____

_____

_____

_____

_____

_____

_____

_____

_____

_____

_____

_____

_____

_____

_____

_____

_____

_____

_____

_____

_____

Chapter 4

Living Room:
The Living Is Easy

Your living room can be a child care activity center without your worrying about dirt, damage, or danger. You can enjoy your living room and use the space efficiently with these ways to stop dirt in its tracks, protect the children's safety, encourage children to help you clean up, and just have fun.

Slip Ons

Every pair of shoes carries twelve pounds of dirt into your home each year! Reduce this amount by asking parents to buy their children soft-soled slippers they can wear in your home. Have children remove their shoes at the door and wear their slippers inside. Keep the slippers at your house.

Dirt Defense

Protect your sofa cushions by making large-sized pillowcases that close with Velcro fastening tape. On weekends, remove and wash.

Quick Cover-Up

If your sofa arm covers are missing, lay a bath towel over the sofa arm. Lift the cushion, and tuck the rest of the towel deep into the side of the sofa. Easy to remove, wash, and replace.

Sofa Storage

Store large art paper under your sofa until you need it. It will lie flat and will also stop other toys from rolling too far under the furniture.

Indoor Gardeners

Keep children away from the dirt in your large planters by covering the soil with pinecones. Air and water pass right through, and the children can't reach the dirt. The pinecones also discourage your cat from using the soil as a litter box.

Record Keeping

Use a plastic crate turned on its side to store record albums. The record player can be set on top so everything is handy and easy to put away. A plastic or cardboard shoe box is great for storing CDs and cassettes. Stack these in the crate.

Freshen Up

Give your living room a pleasant smell by sprinkling a few drops of liquid potpourri on the disposable paper bag in your vacuum cleaner. The smell will fill the room as you vacuum.

Lemon "Aid"

Fill a clean plastic lemon juice squeezer with paint the same color as your living room walls. When a touch-up is needed, just squeeze a little paint onto a cosmetic cotton square or a cotton swab and daub the paint on the wall. Keep the lemon out of children's reach.

Safety First

Although your living room poses fewer dangers than other areas of your home, some safety hazards may go unnoticed until it's too late. To prevent possible problems, plug child-proof covers into all electrical outlets. Be sure heating vents, radiators, and space heaters have guards to protect children from burns. And be sure safety gates do not have V- or diamond-shaped openings that could trap a child's head. If you have houseplants, be sure they are out of children's reach. Along with these tips, the following ideas will help you keep the living room safer for the children in your care.

Wrap it Up

Wrap lamp cords around table legs to prevent tod-dlers from pulling over the lamp. The shortened cords also prevent tripping.

Cordless Homes

Use spring-type clothespins to secure drapery or mini-blind cords out of children's reach. Just clip the cord to the inside of the drape or onto a slat of the blinds.

Keep Away

Place one or two playpens (with or without children in them) in front of your unlit fireplace to discourage children from climbing on or running toward a raised hearth and risking injury.

See-Through Safety

Use press-on decals with seasonal designs on sliding glass patio doors. Place the decals at children's eye level to delight them and make everyone aware of the glass.

Stable Table

Babies who are starting to walk can push coffee tables into other furniture. Put rubber crutch tips on the bottom of the coffee table legs to make moving the table more difficult.

On the Right Track

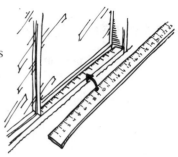

Prevent children from shutting your sliding glass patio door on someone's fingers. Lay a yardstick in the track to keep the door open. (Use a ruler if you want the door open only a foot.)

It's in the Bag

During cold and flu season, tape a paper bag to the wall or door high enough so toddlers can't tear it down. To help control the spread of germs, challenge the children to make a basket with their used tissues. Dirty tissues end up in the "germ basket," and no one needs to handle them.

Stay Inside

Keep sliding glass patio doors closed with a rubber-tipped, spring-tension rod. Place it high enough so that you can reach it, but children can't. The rod will keep children from going outside without your knowledge.

Helping Hands

Children will help clean up if you make the activity fun. Use these tips to turn routine tasks into mini-adventures.

Clearly Fun

Make a game of cleaning fingerprints off the glass in doors and windows. Cover the children's hands with cotton socks and spray a little vinegar on the glass. Let the kids "rub-a-dub" until it sparkles.

Fetch a Pail of Clutter

Save large plastic ice cream pails with handles and give one to each child at cleanup time. Give the children responsibility for filling their pails and putting away the contents.

House Detectives

If a puzzle piece or toy part is missing, offer a reward. You'll be surprised how quickly it's found.

Treasure Hunt

When it's time to clean up, assign "pirates" to look for certain treasures. Tell Eric to search for all the toys with wheels, Becky to hunt for all the dolls, and Meredith to find all the books. When they've unearthed their treasures and stowed them away, invite them to the galley for a snack.

Just Like Mommy

Children love to use adult tools, so let them take turns vacuuming the living room. The job won't be perfect, but it will be okay, and the children will have fun. Be sure everyone gets a turn; record who did what on a chart.

Going Home Fun

Thirty minutes before closing time, select two or three non-messy activities (such as reading books and assembling puzzles) to be done at the kitchen or dining room table after everything else is put away. Enjoy the table activities while parents are picking up their children. When everyone is gone, clear the books and puzzles from the table, walk into your tidy living room, and put up your feet.

Living Room Fun

You and the children will have more fun in your living room if you establish boundaries and ground rules. These tips will help you avoid damage and keep quarreling to a minimum.

No Toys Allowed

Your sofa cushions can swallow small toys, never to be seen again! Use the sofa only for reading books and playing with dolls. Tell children to play with other toys on the floor or on tables.

Puzzle Place

Use your coffee table for a puzzle-working surface. Turn over a plastic table-cloth, flannel-side up, and cover the table. Secure corners with spring-type clothespins or sew down the corners to make a fitted cover.

Crawl Space

Create a hiding place behind a large chair by removing plants, floor lamps, and electrical cords. Let this be the children's special place and ask them not to crawl behind the other furniture.

Sound-Off

Protect your entertainment center by surrounding it with a multiple-sectioned hinged play yard. The barrier will keep small children from trying the buttons on stereos and televisions.

 IMPORTANT SAFETY TIP:

Never use expandable play yards that have V- or diamond-shaped openings, which could trap a child's head.

Assigned Seats

Avoid quarreling over who sits where in your living room. Assign places and rotate them daily so everyone can enjoy the favorite spots. Be sure to save a spot for yourself.

Snuggle Up

If all the children want to sit together on your lap when you snuggle into a big chair to read, help them take turns by naming a special child of the day. Use a garter-type armband to designate which child gets the privilege for the day. Use your calendar to keep track and be sure everyone gets a turn.

Just for You

Mail Call

Set aside five minutes to read your mail by sitting on your sofa and placing a pillow beside you. Teach the children the pillow means you are in a "good" time-out. Set your kitchen timer for five minutes. The children will know this is your special time, and you'll be able to read your mail undisturbed.

Your Own Ideas

Use this space to write your own living room fun and safety ideas. To find out how to share your ideas, see appendix B.

_____

_____

_____

_____

_____

_____

_____

_____

_____

_____

_____

_____

_____

_____

_____

Chapter 5

Bedroom:

A Place for Snorin' and Storin'

Naps are important for young children, and well-rested children are more fun to be around. When you use your bedrooms for the children's naptime, be sure they don't get into mischief when they're supposed to be resting. The ideas in this chapter offer ways to darken rooms, keep roommates from disturbing each other, create storage areas, keep children safe, and enhance children's physical and emotional comfort.

High and Dry

Protect your family's mattresses from bed-wetting accidents at naptime. Use a large flannel-backed plastic tablecloth. Place it flannel-side up between the bedspread and the child's naptime bedding. Fold and store under the bed after naps.

Sleep On It

A crib-sized mattress placed on the floor makes a wonderful napping cot for children up to the age of six.

Down Under

The floor space under your family's beds is a good place to store naptime cots or plastic-covered mattresses when not in use.

 IMPORTANT SAFETY TIP:

To ensure cleanliness and prevent contamination, army-type cots or uncovered mattresses should not be used in child care.

Lighten Your Load

Ask each parent to bring a clean blanket, pillowcase, and fitted crib sheet each Monday. Send bedding home to be laundered at the end of the week. Children rest better when their bedclothes smell like home, and you'll lighten your laundry load.

Time's Up

Preschoolers who sleep in the same room can't resist a little chitchat before falling asleep. Set a kitchen timer for five minutes and let them visit. When the timer rings, it's time to sleep.

Roommate Rule

Older children who are reluctant to sleep can rest in the same room with toddlers. Tell them they can look at books once younger children are asleep. If older children are tired, they'll fall asleep waiting for the others to nap. If not, they'll be quiet waiting for the chance to enjoy the books.

Something To Look Up To

A colorful poster on the ceiling above the changing table or crib will entertain a baby during diapering.

Sound Off

Turn off the ringer on your bedroom phone during naptime. You'll still be able to hear other phones ring, but sleeping children won't be disturbed.

Book Hook

Hang a clipboard or spiral notebook from a plastic hook attached to the outside of the crib. Record diaper changes, naps, and other information about the baby's day for yourself or the baby's parents.

 IMPORTANT SAFETY TIP:

Be sure the hook is out of the baby's reach.

Lights Out

If you don't have a room-darkening shade, drape an old mattress pad or blanket over the top of the bedroom curtain rod to block light at naptime. Secure with spring-type clothespins.

Private Rooms

Use a cardboard pattern-cutting board from a fabric store to give children who sleep on cots or mats more privacy. Cut the board in half lengthwise. Fold in thirds on precut folds. You now have two bedroom walls that will each stand up around the head of a cot or mat. The boards fold flat for storage. Children can use markers to personalize their "rooms."

Bag It

Use a six-compartment shoe bag hung on the outside of the crib to store baby's necessities.

A La Carte

Use a three-sectioned laundry cart to store three babies' personal diapers, clothes, and bedding. Use one section for each child to avoid getting items mixed up.

Pack it Up

Ask parents to bring bedding and nap toys in a backpack or canvas bag marked with the child's name. After naptime, put the sheet, blanket, and toy in the backpack or bag until the next day. You can also use the backpack or bag to send home bedding for laundering. This tip will help you comply with health regulations that require keeping children's bedding separate.

Stowaways

Store children's naptime needs in a no-longer-used bassinet.

Out of Sight

A baby crib dust ruffle creates an out-of-sight storage area for crib sheets and diapers. Store items in laundry baskets to keep them off the floor.

Safety First

Be sure the children stay safe when you tuck them in for naps. Use these tips to keep an eye on sleeping children and prevent injured fingers from closet doors or electric fans.

Listen Up

Don't put away your baby monitor when the babies in your care become toddlers. Use it at naptime for all ages.

Keep it Shut

Secure sliding closet doors by placing a rubber-tipped tension curtain rod between the outer door and the closet door frame.

No Trespassing

Lock bedrooms where you do not want the children to go during the day using a small lock near the top on the outside of the door. A pivot door lock works well. Ask for one at a hardware store.

Open Door Policy

A towel draped over the top of the bedroom door keeps it from closing all the way. You can check on sleeping children without waking them up when opening the door. Keep door hinges oiled to prevent squeaks.

Open Door Policy II

If an open bedroom door lets too much light into the room, but you don't want to close it during naps, hang a curtain from a tension rod in the doorway. Sew several jingle bells inside the curtain hem so you'll know if a toddler is escaping.

 IMPORTANT SAFETY TIP:

Be sure bells are secured inside the hem to prevent them from becoming a choking hazard.

Rock, But Don't Roll

To keep babies from rocking a crib across the floor, remove the casters and set the crib legs on rubber furniture protectors.

It's a Breeze

If you use fans to cool a room, keep them where children can't reach. As an added precaution, make a cover with nylon net and elastic. For a small fan, use a lady's mesh curler cap. Slip it over the face of the fan. Air will pass through, but fingers won't.

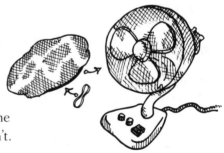

Comfort Zones

Children sleep better when they're physically and emotionally comfortable. Set a daily routine, so when it's time for naps, the children will be used to lying down without complaints. A well-rested child is less likely to be fussy, so follow these tips for helping children rest.

Snuggle Buddies

Encourage each child to bring a comfort toy from home for naptime. When children arrive, have them put the toy on the bed where they will sleep. Tell them their "Boo Bear" will be waiting to snuggle with them later.

Warm-Ups

For winter comfort, put children's blankets in the dryer for ten minutes to warm them just before naptime.

Picture This

A large laminated picture of a parent placed within a baby's view may reduce fussing at naptime.

Now Hear This

A child going through separation anxiety can be soothed by a parent's voice at naptime. Ask the parents to tape themselves singing a lullaby, reading a story, or just talking to the child. Play the tape when you put the child down for a nap.

Now Hear This II

Classical music is soothing; play it during naptime so the children can hear it faintly in the bedrooms.

Just for You

Music to My Dears

Place a stereo, tape player, or CD player and your favorite music in the room where the children sleep. After putting them down, turn on the music. It will soothe the children and give you time to unwind. Lie down yourself and relax for 15 to 20 minutes. Soon the music will become a signal for the children to sleep.

Your Own Ideas

Use this space to write your own naptime comfort and bedroom storage ideas.
To find out how to share your ideas, see appendix B.

Chapter 6

Bathroom:

More than Flushin' and Brushin'

How do you store razors and aerosols out of the children's reach? What's a good way to keep the toilet bowl clean? How can you keep children from pumping too much liquid soap out of the dispenser? This chapter includes ideas that make bathroom activities easier for the children. It also includes tips for safety, storage, and cleaning.

Common Scents

To encourage hand washing, try this idea. Use small, different colored "pretty" soaps and put one on each side of the bathroom sink. Tell the children you want to try to guess which soap they used by smelling their clean hands. They will often use both soaps to try to throw you off the scent. The results are fun—and very clean hands.

Art Space

After children have painted pictures, lay the drawings flat to dry on the bottom of your bathtub. Paint splatters can be easily rinsed away after the pictures go home with your budding artists.

Step into my Office

If your home is small, you may need to use your bathroom as a conference room when a child is upset and needs private comforting or when you need to talk to a child about negative behavior. Sit on the edge of the tub so you're at the child's eye level. This is an ideal place to soothe the child with a cool facecloth and quiet conversation away from curious others.

Wash and Dry

Washcloths are large enough for children to use to dry their hands and faces. Sew or hot glue buttons of different colors or shapes on corners of individual washcloths. Then make a chart and glue a matching button beside each child's name. A red button next to Christopher's name means the cloth with the red button is his. For a variation, use the same idea, but buy different colors of washcloths. Color-code your chart using markers or pieces of colored paper.

 IMPORTANT SAFETY TIP:

Be sure buttons are securely fastened to avoid a choking hazard.

Button Up

Individual hand towels with crocheted tops that loop over and button can be used over a towel bar in the bathroom. Perhaps one of the children's grand-mothers would make some for you, if you buy the supplies.

 IMPORTANT SAFETY TIP:

Be sure buttons are securely fastened to avoid a choking hazard.

Toothbrush Stand Up

Store toothbrushes by standing them upright in a can of unpopped popcorn ker-nels. The brushes will be able to air dry without touching each other.

 IMPORTANT SAFETY TIP:

Keep out of children's reach to avoid a choking hazard.

Hang-Ups

Hang a skirt rack with pinch clips from your towel bar to hang children's washcloths to dry.

Hang-Ups II

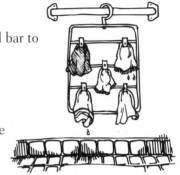

Place an expandable laundry drying rack inside the bathtub to hang up children's hand towels.

Hang-Ups III

Attach an expandable mug rack to the inside of the bathroom door at the children's level. Children can easily reach their own towels or washcloths.

Yipes! Pipes!

Use an old pipe rack to store children's toothbrushes. Paint it to match your bathroom.

Rack 'em Up

A man's tie rack makes a handy toothbrush holder. Suspend the toothbrushes from the holes in the brush handles.

One at a Time

Children have trouble tearing off just one sheet of paper toweling. Have your helper of the day tear sheets from a roll and turn up the corner of each one. Stack the sheets in a basket with the corners sticking up so children can take just one towel at a time.

Out of the Way

Store your diaper pail inside your bathtub or shower stall during child care hours. You'll have more floor space in the bathroom, and you'll keep inquisitive children away from this source of germs. Also, you'll be able to wash your hands immediately after depositing the dirty diaper.

Clean Care Cart

Create a clean care station with a three-tiered cart. Set it on a clean beach towel laid on the bottom of the bathtub. Use magnetic clips around the edge to hang the children's towels. On top place different colored plastic mugs for children to use and store their toothbrushes and toothpaste. Use the second and third shelves for stacking items such as diapers and clean towels, wipes, and extra toilet tissue.

Easy Cleaning

Keep your toilet bowl clean by pouring in 1/4 cup of bleach each night before you go to bed.

 IMPORTANT SAFETY TIPS:

Flush the toilet before children arrive. Always store bleach and chemicals away in locked cabinets where children cannot reach them.

Hats Off

While children wash their hands and face, have them place their drying cloths on their heads. The towels are within easy reach when needed.

Highchair Car Wash

Clean sticky highchairs and booster seats in your shower. Run hot water over them for five minutes, then turn them upside down for another five minutes. Even crusty gunk wipes right off with an old bath towel.

Pop Ups

If toddlers insist on unrolling toilet tissue, remove the roll and place a box of plain pop-up facial tissues on top of the toilet tank to use instead of toilet tissue.

Pump it Up

If you like the convenience of pump soap, but the children pump out too much, wrap a rubber band around the neck of the pump to minimize the amount of soap dispensed.

Safety First

Prevent falls and hot water burns, keep dangerous items like razors away from children, and avoid accidental lock-ins with these easy safety tips.

Mirror, Mirror

To keep children from climbing onto the sink to see themselves in the mirror, hang a mirror down low where they'll have easy access. This idea encourages them to wash their faces, too.

Fresh Squeeze

Avoid hot water burns by covering your hot water tap with an empty plastic lemon (the kind lemon juice comes in). Cut one-fourth off the bottom of the lemon and force it onto your hot water tap. You're strong enough to squeeze the lemon and turn on the hot water, but the children's hands are too small to squeeze hard enough.

Keep Away

Shampoos, conditioners, razors, and other personal care products become hazards when left on the bathtub ledge or vanity. Keep them away from children, but within easy reach of your family members by suspending a three-tiered wire basket in the corner of the shower away from the showerhead.

Lock Up

To avoid having to remove your family's personal care items from the bathroom medicine cabinet, install a lock over the top of the cabinet where only you and other adult family members can unlock it.

 IMPORTANT SAFETY TIP:

Be sure the cabinet stays locked during child care hours.

Lock Out

To keep children from locking themselves in the bathroom, disengage your bathroom lock. Install a sliding lock or gate lock on the inside, high enough for your family's privacy.

Lock Out II

To keep children from locking the bathroom door, tie a loop in one end of a nylon stocking. Fit the loop over the inside of the doorknob. Stretch the nylon tight enough to cover the door latch so it can't lock. Tie the other end of the stocking over the outside doorknob.

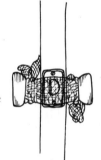

Lock Out III

Throw a towel over the top of the bathroom door to keep it from closing completely.

Potty Pennies

Children are attracted to water—even the water in your toilet bowl. Encourage potty-trained children to put down the toilet lid by creating a reward system. Drop a penny in a piggy bank each time they remember to flush, put down the lid, and wash their hands. When you have enough pennies, buy a special book or puzzle everyone can enjoy.

 IMPORTANT SAFETY TIP:

Coins can be a choking hazard, so be sure to store the bank out of children's reach.

Just for You

Now Smell This

When you feel stressed, lift your spirits by wetting a facecloth with cool water then spritzing it with your favorite cologne. Gently pat your face, neck, and arms.

 IMPORTANT SAFETY TIP:

Lock the cologne in your medicine cabinet, out of children's sight and reach.

Your Own Ideas

Use this space to write your own bathroom safety and storage ideas. To find out how to share your ideas, see appendix B.

_____

_____

_____

_____

_____

_____

_____

_____

_____

_____

_____

_____

_____

Chapter 7

Closets:
New Faces for Tight Spaces

If child care toys, supplies, clothes, and bedding seem to have taken over your home, use these ideas for more efficient storage in closets and cubbies. Use suitcases to get a grip on child care storage problems. And don't overlook closet doors, which can increase your storage space.

Stow Away

Dedicate a closet to your child care toys and games. Remove the clothes bar, and add shelving. Use sturdy plastic containers on top shelves for infrequently used items, such as holiday decorations, water toys, and seasonal books and tapes. Also use top shelves to store special games that you must give permission to bring out. Use sturdy dishpans to store cars, trucks, blocks, and other toys. At the end of the day, everything is put away, and your home is tidy.

Lay Away

An old changing table tucked into a closet makes a great place to store toys, books, and games.

Keep Out

To keep small children from getting into a
toy closet, place a baby gate in the closet
doorway. Older children can reach over it to
get the toys they want, but crawling babies
won't be able to pull games with small
pieces off the shelves. Babies stay safe from
choking hazards, and your toy closet shelves
stay neat.

 IMPORTANT SAFETY TIP:

*Never use baby gates that have V- or diamond-shaped openings, which could trap a
child's head.*

Inventory Control

Use a number code to identify contents of hard-to-reach storage containers.
Mark each box or storage container with a number. Then write an inventory list
to post inside the closet door.

Rack 'em Up

If your coat closet is too full or you don't have one near the door, make a coat
rack from a wooden changing table. Attach blunt screw hooks to the sides for
the children's coats. Use the shelves to store diaper bags and backpacks. Shoes
and boots fit underneath. Keep the top free and use it to change diapers. You
can move the table to a bedroom for the weekend.

Everything in its Place

Every Friday afternoon bring toy containers out of the closet. Let the children
help you put all the toys in their proper places for the coming week.

Art To Go

Store art supplies in a suitcase. Be sure to hang an identifying tag on the outside
to help you remember which suitcase you put the supplies in.

What's Inside?

Make a hanging tag for storage boxes
and other containers to identify contents. Make a sturdy tag from a piece of
plastic cut from the side of a milk jug and use
a hole punch or ice pick to make a hole.
Write on the tag with a permanent marker
and attach it to the storage box with a string.

It's in the Mail

Large rural mailboxes make inexpensive cubbies for belongings children leave at
your home. Line mailboxes across the top of a low bookcase and put the children's names on the doors. Secure to the top of the bookcase with screws on the
inside of the mailboxes. Put up the red flag when there's something inside that
the child needs to take home.

 IMPORTANT SAFETY TIP:

Anchor the bookcase to the wall.

Odor Control

Your closet will smell nice if you buy a bag of cedar chips. Get the kind sold for
gerbil cages. Punch a few holes in the top so the fragrance can escape. Then
place the bag on a top closet shelf, out of reach of "helping" hands.

Garment Bags

Use your stored suitcases to keep dress-up clothes from getting wrinkled and
messy. Use one suitcase for girls' clothes and one for boys'. Teach children to
fold clothes carefully when "packing."

Jewelry Case

Use an old-style train case from a thrift shop or garage sale to store dress-up
jewelry. To store suitcases, put small ones inside large ones to save space.

Opening Acts

Closet doors offer more than a way to hide whatever is inside. The outside of the door can be a message center, and you can use the inside of the door for storing anything from family jackets to your canister vacuum cleaner.

Lights Out

If your closet light has a pull chain, lengthen the cord so children can turn the light on and off without your help. Put screw eyes on the inside door frame (one toward the top of the door frame; one midway between the top and the floor). Thread the pull-chain through the screw eyes. At the children's height, add a sturdy pull larger than the screw eyes.

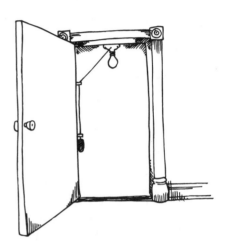

Mirror, Mirror

Use the inside of your closet door to store dress-up clothes. Hang a full-length mirror (child-height) on the inside of the door. On the rest of the door's surface, install blunt plastic hooks to hang the clothes on.

Message Center

A logical place for a parents' message center is the outside of the closet door where you keep the children's coats. Mount a bulletin board turned lengthwise on the door and use a 3-by-5-inch index card for each child's name. Leave space under each name card where you can thumbtack reminders like "Remember Johanna's medicine in the refrigerator." Be sure to include a card that says "All Parents." Use this space to post information and reminders that apply to everyone.

Hang-Ups

If you have lots of jackets to hang up, try this. Hang an over-the-door clothes arm to hold jackets that belong to family members. The bottom two-thirds of the door is still available for an expandable mug rack that the children in your care can reach to hang their coats and jackets.

Hang-Ups II

Hang your canister vacuum cleaner on the inside of a closet door. A laundry bag hanging next to it can hold your attachments.

Spare Change

Keep the children's changes of clothes in a diaper stacker inside a closet door. Extra shirts and pants stay neat, and you'll always know where to find them.

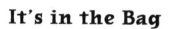

It's in the Bag

Hang a multi-pocket shoe bag on the inside of a closet door to store children's mittens, hats, and scarves.

Lock Out

Children like to hide in closets. If any of your closet doors can be locked from the inside, be sure to disable the locks.

Just for You

Hideaway

Hang an old purse in the back of a closet on a high hook. Like a squirrel saving nuts for winter, save money each week and hide it in the purse. At the end of the month (or year) buy something special for yourself.

Your Own Ideas

Use this space to write your own closet uses and storage ideas. To find out how to share your ideas, see appendix B.

Chapter 8

Office:
Mind Over Scatter

Record-keeping will be easier with these tips for office supplies, furnishings, and storage. There are even tips for what to do if you don't have a spare room to use for an office. A three-hole punch, three-ring binder, calculator, paper, and pencil can be all you need to keep child care records. These ideas will help you keep files and supplies handy so you can stay organized.

Tax Facts

Good record-keeping prevents tax-time nightmares. Use the twelve-file, twenty-four-envelope method to simplify record-keeping: Label a file folder for each month of the year. Then label two envelopes for each month, writing "cash" on one and "checks" on the other. Carry the two envelopes in your purse throughout the month. Use them for receipts for child care-related expenses. At the time of purchase, write "cash" or your check number on the receipt and put the receipt in the proper envelope before you leave the store. At the end of the month, file the envelopes in that month's folder so you'll know where they are when tax time arrives.

One Day at a Time

Because family child care is a business, you need time to keep your records in order. While children nap, use fifteen to twenty minutes each day to keep up on your office work. Doing a little each day keeps papers from piling up.

Stock Up

When you set up your child care office, buy all the supplies you need. Keep them in a desk drawer. (If they're on top of the desk, they're too tempting!) Teach your family not to borrow your business tools. You'll need stamps, pens, pencils, scissors, a three-hole punch, paper clips, rubber bands, scratch paper, spiral notebooks, tape and dispenser, letter opener, correction fluid, file folders with labels, stapler with extra staples, and other assorted supplies. Keep your receipts for these supplies for tax time.

Mail Call

Open all your mail at your desk and—at that moment—file or toss out. Put important "to pay" notations on your calendar. You'll stay organized and keep down clutter.

Date Line

Keep a calendar over or near your desk to remind you of important dates. Use stick-on stars for the children's birthdays, smiley face stickers for the day you mail in your food program menus, and special stickers for field trip days or training sessions. Check the calendar daily.

To Do Lists

Keep a "to do" clipboard on your desk and list jobs that need your attention. It's satisfying to cross off your accomplishments.

Dedicated Drawer

If you use your desk for family affairs as well as for your child care business, label one file drawer "Child Care" so other work doesn't clutter your business records.

Mail Order

If you order something by mail, record the date and company address in your daily journal. You'll have ready access in case you need to follow up on the order.

Dear Diary

Keep a daily journal just for your child care business. Write in it every day and record details like Alex's falling off a swing, Elizabeth's chicken pox, or the date a child comes to or leaves your child care. There may come a time when you'll need this information, and you'll have a permanent record that's easy to find.

Check it Out

Open a checking account exclusively for your child care business. Having a separate account saves having to write "child care" on the memo line of each check, and you won't have to go through your personal account at year's end.

Cash In

Each payday set aside some petty cash to use for child care-related items. Keep the cash in an envelope in your purse and use for small child care incidentals and garage sale purchases.

Color Code

Use colored file folders for the children's medical records. They'll be easier to find if you need them in a hurry.

Card Shop

Buy children's birthday and get well cards in advance and keep them in your desk. You'll save time and won't panic if you temporarily forget someone's special day.

Addresses on File

Use rotating file cards or a box with 3-by-5-inch index cards to keep track of all your child care-related addresses and phone numbers.

Addresses To Go

Buy a small address book to carry in your purse. Include the children's birthdays, home addresses, home phone numbers, and parents' work numbers. If you need this information while you're on a field trip, you'll have it with you.

Long Distance Log

Use a small spiral notebook to keep track of your child care-related long distance calls. Record the date, time, and person called and compare with your phone bill for accuracy. Save your list of itemized calls from your long distance company. At tax time, you'll have a complete record.

Stick-On Addresses

Order preprinted adhesive-backed address labels and use them on all correspondence. You can also use them to identify your office supplies so you can relocate items family members borrow.

Stick-On Addresses II

Ask all the children's parents to give you two of their address labels. Put one in the address book you carry in your purse. Below the label put both parents' work phone numbers. Use the other label on the child's file. Ask for new labels if the family moves. Stick the new ones over the old ones.

I.D. Stamp

Order a self-inking rubber stamp with your name and address to stamp your return address on envelopes or to identify books and other items.

Create an Office

A closet, bookcase, or a simple expandable file can serve as your child care business office. Follow these tips to create office space where none seems to exist.

Closet Conversion

You can convert a closet into a mini-office. Place a small desk in the closet with a chair that will push under it. Remove the clothes bar and install shelves to within 6 inches of the top of your head when you are seated. Use an extension cord dropped from the overhead closet light to plug in a desk lamp or other electrical equipment. Install a lock high on the outside of the door.

Space Case

If you don't have a spare room to use for an office, use a low bookcase to create a wall. Place the bookcase near a corner at a 90 degree angle to the wall of the room, leaving space the width of your desk. Slide your desk into position and plug in your desk lamp.

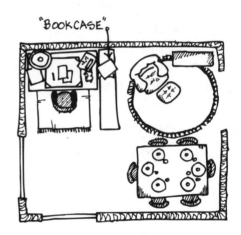

"BOOKCASE"

 IMPORTANT SAFETY TIP:

Be sure to anchor the bookcase.

Office To Go

Buy a "desk side file" on wheels at an office supply store. Use it as a rolling office that you can move to wherever you find it convenient to work. Get one that holds hanging files and also has a lower shelf you can use to store office supplies. Use a tackle box for small supplies.

 IMPORTANT SAFETY TIP:

Be sure to lock it away during child care hours so children won't get into potentially dangerous objects like staplers and scissors.

Mini-Office

Make a desk that serves as a complete office. Buy two two-drawer metal file cabinets and an unfinished wood door. Paint, stain, or varnish the door. Space the files apart the length of the door and set the door on top. Use contact cement from the hardware store to anchor the door to the cabinets. Add a desk lamp, slide a secretary's chair underneath, and you're all set.

Mini-Office II

If you don't have room for a desk, buy two molded plastic crates. Use one for hanging files. Store office supplies in the other. Store in a closet or convenient corner out of reach of "helping" hands.

Mini-Office III

If you can't afford a metal file cabinet, buy a cardboard one at an office supply store. Get a two-drawer model. Use one drawer for files and the other for your office supplies.

IMPORTANT SAFETY TIP:

Store away from children's reach.

On the Record

If space is limited, you can use an expandable file for your business records. Mark the year on the outside and label each divider with a different month. Keep receipts and other papers filed according to date.

Just for You

Dreamin'

Create a file where you save clippings of redecorating items, clothes, sports equipment, or vacation spots you'd like to visit. Each payday go through your file and dream about what you're working so hard to earn.

Your Own Ideas

Use this space to write your own office and record-keeping ideas. To find out how to share your ideas, see appendix B.

Chapter 9

Playroom/ Basement:

No Work and All Play

Every family child care home needs a place for children to play indoors. Whether you use a ground-level playroom or a basement that meets local safety requirements, you can use the ideas in this chapter to make your playroom more efficient. The tips help you store toys, arrange furnishings, repair playpens, and make useful items out of things intended to be used for something else. See special headings for basement fun, safety tips, and ways to encourage children to help with chores and cleanups.

On the Line

Display artwork by stringing a length of fishing line across the room. Attach drawings with tape. (Clothespins are too heavy; they'll make the line sag.)

It's in the Bag

Secure a six-pocket shoe bag inside the playpen and fill each compartment with a rattle or another baby toy. The baby will enjoy practicing "putting in" and "taking out."

Flying High

Suspend several colorful kites from the ceiling to brighten your playroom.

Hang-Ups

Attach an 18-inch chrome towel bar to the back of the playroom door. Use spring-type clothespins to hang artwork to dry.

Cover-Ups

Make covers for playpen pads out of a twin-sized bedsheet. Cut the sheet in half and make a pillowcase-type cover. Close with Velcro fastening tape. The sheet is easy to remove for washing, and you'll increase the life of your pad.

A Stitch in Time

Repair small holes in playpen mesh right away. Use fishing line or dental floss to close the hole. Strengthen the repair by weaving the line or floss three or four holes past the tear.

On Edge

Make a new decorative rim around the edge of a worn playpen top with a flannel-backed vinyl tablecloth. Cut to fit, then sew it on by hand using fishing line or dental floss.

See-Through Storage

Store Lego plastic building blocks, Tinkertoy building blocks, and other toys with small pieces in clear plastic containers. The playroom will stay tidy, and children will be able to see what's inside without opening the boxes.

It's a Long Story

Use a long extension cord on your vacuum cleaner to avoid repeated trips to unplug and plug in the cord.

Dolly Trolly

If children need a way to move a heavy box of building blocks, have them use a mechanic's creeper (the wooden or plastic board mechanics use to lie on and roll under cars). Children can use it as a dolly to pull the blocks to the building site and return them to their proper place when construction is complete. To save floor space, store the mechanics creeper and blocks under a table when not in use.

Border Wars

Preschoolers like to build, and toddlers like to knock down. Give both age groups space to play in the same room by creating a barrier with available furniture or playpens. Everyone will be happier.

Boundary Lines

Create activity centers by attaching masking tape along the floor. The tape peels right up when you're finished.

Boundary Lines II

Create activity centers in your playroom with sturdy, used coffee tables (find them at garage sales). Put a box of different toys or activity center supplies near or under each table.

Pull Up a Chair

Use stackable molded plastic step stools in assorted colors as seats for low, child-sized tables. Children can easily move them or carry them to a reading circle for story time.

Hang 'em High

Store plush toys in a hammock in the corner of the playroom.

All the World's a Stage

Throw a blanket over a tension rod in the playroom doorway, and you have an instant backdrop or stage curtain for a puppet show.

Indoor Zoo

For hours of creative play, form a three-sided zoo cage using strong cord or rope to tie together three baby gates you no longer use. Children can easily crawl in and out.

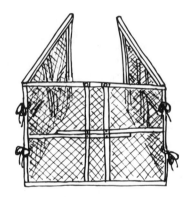

 IMPORTANT SAFETY TIP:

Never use baby gates that have V- or diamond-shaped openings, which could trap a child's head.

Animal Antics

An old wooden playpen makes a fun animal cage. Remove the bottom and unhinge one side. Children will have hours of fun using their imaginations.

Roll Stoppers

Use non-slip bathroom strips on shelves where you store toys with wheels. The strips will keep the toys from rolling off.

Roll Stoppers II

Older children enjoy games and building sets with small pieces that can roll off a table and pose a choking hazard for younger children. Place those toys on trays or cookie sheets with sides to contain the small pieces. Have the older children play with them on a table away from the younger children.

Toy Time-Out

When children are fighting over a toy or using one too roughly, put the toy in time-out for a few minutes. Explain respect for property to the children. Then demonstrate how to use it properly and reintroduce it into play.

Piece "Meal"

Keep game pieces together by using a clean pizza box to replace a game box that is falling apart. Label the outside of the box.

Imagination Station

Store toys on shelves instead of in a toy box. Let children use the toy box (with lid removed) for a boat, race car, house, or whatever their imaginations create.

 IMPORTANT SAFETY TIP:

Remove hinged toy box lids before using a toy box for child care. A heavy lid poses danger to children.

Sleeping Quarters

If you have standard cots with lightweight aluminum frames, use them to create a fun hideout during playtime. Just lean the cots against the wall at an angle and let children crawl behind them.

Stack 'em Up

Several stackable napping cots provide a child-height surface children can use as a doll bed, store counter, or puzzle work area.

 IMPORTANT SAFETY TIP:

Army-type cots should not be used in child care.

Taking Turns

Use Sweetheart Place Cards (see chapter 2) to draw names for taking turns with toys or to decide who goes first when playing a board game.

Something Completely Different

Use your creative energy to turn items that might otherwise be discarded into useful items for your family child care playroom. Design and make items out of inexpensive materials or objects originally designed for other uses.

Round and Round We Go

With your help, an obsolete record player becomes an art center for beautiful spin art. Remove the arm and set the turntable inside a deep cardboard box. (Make a hole near the bottom of the back side for the cord.) Cut a piece of heavy art paper 1 inch larger than the record player's turntable. Punch a hole in the center and place it over the spindle. Turn on the switch and let children dribble different colors of tempera paint onto the spinning paper.

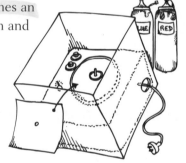

 IMPORTANT SAFETY TIP:

Only an adult should run the record player.

Grounded Walker

Walkers are considered unsafe. If you have one, you can recycle it by removing the wheels and letting the children use it as a doll's highchair.

Sound Off

Control noise and fingerprints on playroom walls with a colorful assortment of carpet samples, available at carpet stores (see appendix A). Mount the pieces halfway up the playroom walls to cushion noise and eliminate dirty surfaces.

Create a Closet

Cloth diaper stackers can store dress-up clothes in the playroom. Put hats and handbags in one, shoes and gloves in another.

Crayon Saver

You can store each child's crayons in a plastic box intended for a bar of soap. Put the eight basic colors inside and label each box with the child's name.

Treasure Chest

Use a plastic fishing tackle box to store dress-up jewelry. Always hook the clasps on the necklaces, and they won't get tangled.

Upside Down

Turn over a playpen with a sturdy bottom and use it as a play surface for building with blocks or playing with race cars. Secure the bottom so it won't fold in.

Playpen Hideout

An open playpen turned on its side makes a fun clubhouse. Build an additional room by clipping a bedsheet to the mesh with clothespins and draping the other end of the sheet over the backs of two kitchen chairs or other furniture.

Playpen Hideout II

If a side of your playpen has been destroyed beyond repair, give it a new use. Remove the netting on the torn side and turn the playpen upside down. Secure the floor, which will be the ceiling of the "house," and you'll have a playhouse children can crawl in and out of.

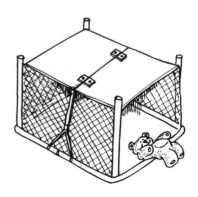

81

Bookcase Cubbies

Playroom shelving can be expensive, so use a bookcase instead. Get one about 6 feet tall. Lay the unit on its side and add cross shelves through the center using plywood cut to fit. You'll have ten or twelve spaces to store toys or belongings.

To increase storage, set the unit on three storage crates (one crate on each end and one in the middle). The crates raise the storage unit high enough to allow air flow from heat and air conditioning vents and keep electric outlets accessible. Wheeled toys can go underneath, and books or record albums will stand up in the crates.

 IMPORTANT SAFETY TIPS:

Anchor the unit to the wall for safety and be sure to cover unused electrical outlets with childproof covers.

Changeable Changing Table

A no-longer-used changing table with square basket-type compartments can serve as a playroom library. Store books for older children on top, and books for smaller children on the bottom. Everyone can now reach the right books.

Goal Shots

Remove the pad from an open playpen. Lay the playpen on its side and use it as a ball return or soccer goal.

Smooth it Over

If your playroom has wall-to-wall carpeting, children won't have a smooth surface for pushing cars or building with blocks. Buy a linoleum remnant for this purpose. Store it under a sofa or playpen so it stays flat when not in use.

Short Stuff

Make an inexpensive play table from an old wooden table (find them at garage sales). Saw off the legs to lower the table to child-height. (Have a four year old sit on a low chair so you can determine the correct table height before you start cutting.) You can also buy old adult-sized wooden chairs and cut down the legs for child-sized furniture at a reasonable price. Paint the tables and chairs bright colors with nontoxic paint to liven up the play area.

Short Stuff II

Create a combination play/work table to share with the children. Buy two two-drawer locking file cabinets and an inexpensive unfin-ished door. Paint or stain the door and lay it across the file cabinets. Use contact cement from the hardware store to anchor the door to the cabinet tops. You'll have a large, low surface where you can sit to plan menus or do child care paperwork while the children draw or work puzzles on the opposite side. One file cabinet is yours, and one is theirs.

Down Under

Your basement can be converted to a playroom or used for storage for your family child care business. Before you use it for child care, though, be sure to check with your licensing agency. Also check city or county zoning regulations and the fire marshall. Whether used for storage or play areas, your underground space will be more efficient with these tips.

Indoor Gardening

Use your basement to start seeds for live-plant gifts for the children's parents. Use easy-to-grow varieties such as marigolds. Place plant cups the children have prepared under a shop light or near a window to sprout. (You'll have to leave on the shop light for seven to eight hours a day.) Let the children check growth only every three or four days so they'll see progress.

Mother Hubbard's Cupboard

Watch for people remodeling kitchens. If they're tearing out old kitchen cupboards or cabinets, ask them to sell—or give—them to you. Mount them in your basement to store stock-up supplies of canned goods or child care items you use only occasionally. Be sure to mount cabinets low enough so you won't need a step stool to get to your supplies.

Toy Store

Use your basement to rotate your toy supply. Put half your playroom toys in storage. Each month, exchange a few of them for toys getting the least attention. Children will be delighted with the "new" toys.

Must Buster

Protect stored items from musty basement odor by buying 30-gallon plastic garbage cans with snap-tight lids. Make inventory tags to hang from the handles so you'll know what's inside.

Ding Dong

If you can't hear your doorbell when you're in the basement, use a baby monitor. Set it near the front door and take the receiver downstairs with you.

 IMPORTANT SAFETY TIPS:

Keep your front door locked at all times, and double-check it whenever you go to the basement. Check with your local fire marshal to be sure you have the kind of lock children can open to escape in case of fire.

Step-By-Step

Check with your licensing agency to see whether you can use colorful carpet remnants from a carpet store to brighten and cushion basement steps.

 IMPORTANT SAFETY TIP:

Be sure to fasten the remnants securely with carpet tacks or follow requirements from your licensing agency.

Kiddie Kitchen

Paint old cupboards and attach low on the wall to create a children's play kitchen. Put a dishpan on one cupboard for a sink. Use a permanent marker to draw stove-top grills on another. Play dishes and pots and pans go inside.

Safety First

Be prepared. Use these tips to reduce the chance of accidents in your playroom and basement and to use your basement as a safe haven from violent storms.

Storm Warnings

Prepare an emergency storm kit. Include a first-aid kit, flashlight, battery-operated radio (check batteries often), roll of paper towels, one-gallon jug of sterile water, paper cups, one can of powdered baby formula, clean baby bottles in Ziploc resealable bags, diapers, wet wipes, a blanket, a hand-operated can opener, a few cans of fruit, beans, and plastic bowls and spoons. Store the items in a laundry basket in the most sheltered area of the basement.

Slam Stopper

Use a sand-filled draft guard on the front side of a door to keep it open. The stopper makes it difficult for a child to slam the door on anyone's fingers.

Quick Getaway

A second exit from your basement can mean the difference between using your basement for a play area and having it off limits. You can install a fire window that meets the code in your area for a reasonable price, depending on how much of the work you do yourself. Check with your local fire marshal and child care licensing agency before you start.

Watch Your Step

Run a line of florescent paint or tape on the first and last basement steps.

Watch Your Step II

Never step over a child gate to go down a set of steps. Your toe can catch on the gate, sending you toppling to the bottom. And stepping over a gate encourages children to do the same.

Watch Your Step III

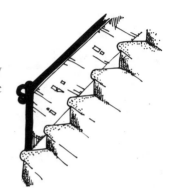

Close off the sides of an open basement stairway by installing sturdy, translucent Plexiglas thermoplastic between the railing and the steps. Light passes through the material so you can see who is coming down or going up.

Calling All Cars

Install an extension telephone in the basement for emergencies. Don't rely on a cordless phone; you're sure to have forgotten to bring it with you when you need it.

Block it Off

Sliding glass patio doors off the basement are potential finger pinchers. Place a small building block in the track as a safety stop.

Run Off

A large open basement area encourages running. Use a sofa or other piece of sturdy furniture to break up the space into activity centers where children can read, play house, or build with blocks.

Padded Poles

Wrap carpet squares around the support poles in the middle of your basement to cushion children who might run into them.

Helping Hands

Children love to help, and when they help in the playroom, chores seem more like games. Try these ways to encourage children to help put away toys, spot spills, sort laundry, and avoid messes during art projects.

Grand Champions

Buy an old trophy at a garage sale and use it to motivate children to pick up toys. Watch as children clean up, then award the trophy to the child who picks up the most, quickest, or most carefully. Award it to a different child every day, for a different reason. Be sure no one is overlooked.

Yipes! Wipes!

Keep a container of moist pop-up wipes in the playroom so children can clean their hands after art projects.

Spill Spotters

Assign spill spotters to alert you when another child spills or spits up on the floor so you can clean it up right away. Give the spotter a reward.

Warm Fuzzies

Children love to help with grown-up activities, so bring warm laundry fresh from the dryer and see who can match socks the fastest. Teach children to fold wash-cloths and towels, too. Talk about color, texture, and size as you work.

Artists in Residence

Place medium-sized paper bags on art tables and use them for trash. Teach older children to clean up their art scraps, put them in the bag, and bring it to you. Older children can enjoy art projects, and babies can't reach the portable wastebaskets.

Just for You

Have a Seat

Invest in a big, soft chair or rocker just for you. Sit there to read, feed a baby, or sing with the children. If a child makes you a special drawing, ask him or her to place it on your chair. Soon the children will understand that they have the rest of the playroom, but the big chair is yours.

Your Own Ideas

Use this space to write your own playroom and basement ideas. To find out how to share your ideas, see appendix B.

_____

_____

_____

_____

_____

_____

_____

_____

_____

_____

_____

_____

_____

_____

Chapter 10

Garage:
Trikes, Bikes...Yikes!

When rainy days keep everyone indoors, the garage can become an out-of-the-weather playground. It's also a good place to store child care items like finished art projects and riding toys. Of course, before you use your garage for child care, be sure lawn mowers, gasoline containers, aerosols, garden poisons, clippers, and other tools and dangerous products are never accessible to children. This chapter includes storage ideas, safety tips, and new uses for garage space. It also includes ideas for your car and tips for trips with children.

Keep Away

Install a secure high shelf in your garage to store paint, grass clippers, pesticides, herbicides, and other dangerous items out of children's reach. Be sure there's nothing under the shelves that children can use to climb on to reach these items.

Drip Dry

Run two or three lengths of clothesline across the garage ceiling to hang drippy paintings, wet swimsuits, or car washing rags. Use old newspapers to absorb the drippings and prevent dangerous puddles.

Recycling Center

Raise money for new child care equipment by establishing a recycling center in your garage. Ask your child care families to donate their empty aluminum cans. Take the cans to a redemption center each week and put the cash in a clear jar so the children can watch the money accumulate. Tape a catalog picture of the item you're saving for to the outside of the jar.

 IMPORTANT SAFETY TIP:

Keep the money out of children's reach to avoid a choking hazard.

Fence Me In

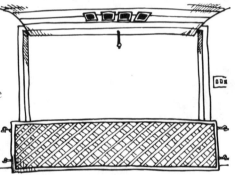

To keep children from wandering away when using your garage for a play area, make a fence from an 8-foot section of garden lattice cut 1 foot longer than the door opening. Secure the lattice in the open doorway with gate hooks on both sides.

Borderline

Form a garden hose into a circle to define a safety border, show children the boundary for a game, or help keep children from getting too close to the door.

 IMPORTANT SAFETY TIP:

Don't rely on the hose to ensure children's safety. Be sure dangerous items are locked or stored out of reach.

Kids' Stuff for Sale—Cheap!

Hold a "kids only" garage sale with donations from your child care families. Sell clothes, toys, books, and other kids' stuff. Have the children help you make signs, sort the items, and sack items customers buy. Use profits to purchase new child care equipment or pay for field trips.

Sand Pit

Fill a heavy-duty molded plastic swimming pool with sand and place in your garage for a winter sandbox.

 IMPORTANT SAFETY TIPS:

Sweep up fallen sand regularly to prevent falls. If you own a cat, cover the sand when not in use.

Swing Away

Hang a porch swing in your garage, and four or five children can enjoy it at the same time. When not in use, pull it back to the wall and suspend it from two large bicycle hanging hooks.

 IMPORTANT SAFETY TIP:

Make a safety bar to go across the front of the swing. Use a sturdy dowel from the hardware store or lumberyard. Screw a gate lock into each end of the dowel and clip the locks onto the vertical chain that goes through the armrest on each side of the swing.

Draft Guards

If cold drafts come in under the door to your garage, use an old vinyl tablecloth to make draft guards. Cut a rectangle 8 inches wide and 2 inches longer than the door width. On the wrong side, sew a seam along the length and one end of the rectangle. (Repeat for extra seam strength.) Turn right-side-out and fill with sand, using a household funnel. Sew the end shut. Lay the draft guard against the bottom of the door to keep out cold air.

Hook Ups

Use "S" bicycle hooks screwed into the garage ceiling crossbeams to hang riding toys, strollers, hula hoops, and other outdoor toys and equipment.

Coat Check

If your garage is attached to your house, ask parents to bring their children in through the garage. Hang coat hooks in the garage beside the door to the house. Parents can remove their children's outerwear, boots, and hats and enjoy a last few minutes together before leaving.

Crossing Guard

When you use your garage and driveway for a play area, place your lawn chair at the street end of the driveway instead of close to the garage. By sitting there, you'll be in a better position to ensure that no child goes into the street, and you can retrieve balls and other toys that get away.

Padded Poles

Wrap carpet squares around the support poles in the middle of your garage to cushion children who might run into them. The squares will also protect your car doors.

Easy Does It!

Tack carpet squares to the garage wall where children open car doors. The carpet will prevent scratches on the doors.

On the Road

If you use your car for field trips or other business trips, these ideas will help driving become safer and more fun. Use other tips to keep track of business expenses and keep the car clean for you and children on the go.

Be Prepared

Always keep an emergency diaper bag in your car. Include diapers, pins, a receiving blanket (which can double as a simple sling), a first-aid kit, copies of the children's emergency medical forms, medical health assessment forms, a list of parents' home and work phone numbers, and change for a pay phone.

Whistle Stops

Hang a whistle from your rear view mirror. Blow it gently to signal time to fasten or unfasten seat belts.

Fast Fastener

Fasten a few toys to the children's car seats with plastic shower curtain rings. The children will have something to amuse themselves with, and the toys won't fall onto the floor of the car.

Stand-Ups

To keep paper grocery bags upright in your van or station wagon, buy two tension rods the width of your vehicle. Space them apart the width of a grocery bag and set bags between them. You can easily remove the rods when you have other items to haul.

Garbage Disposal

An empty three-gallon ice cream pail with a lid makes a convenient car waste basket for messy items like half-eaten ice cream cones and leftover drinks. The mess won't leak onto your upholstery. The pail will also come in handy if a child gets carsick.

Trip Log

Keep a small spiral notebook in the glove compartment to record mileage when you take children to school, parks, and field trips. Also keep track of mileage to get child care groceries and other supplies. At year's end, you'll have records you need for your tax return.

Sing Along

Keep several children's audiocassettes in the car to play while you drive. Sing along with the children to calm crying infants and distract fussy toddlers.

Expense Account

Keep a receipt book in your glove compartment to keep track of child care items you buy at garage sales. Jot down what you buy, the date, and the price. Put the completed receipts in the receipt envelope you carry in your purse.

Dig Out

In winter you can use your empty three-gallon ice cream pail to clear snow from around your tires if you get stuck.

Cover-Ups

In summer keep beach towels in the car to drape over car seats when not in use. The towels will keep the seats and buckles from getting too hot. (They can get hot enough to burn a child's tender skin.)

Cover-Ups II

In summer use a toilet lid cover or fitted crib or bassinet sheet to cover your steering wheel when you park in the hot sun. You'll be able to drive away without burning your hands.

Cool Down

In summer carry a small spray bottle of water in the car. Spray hot seat belt buckles for a quick cool down before fastening.

Yipes! Wipes!

Keep a flat pack of wet wipes in your glove compartment. Keep the children's hands clean, and your car's upholstery will stay clean, too.

Kids on the Go

Order preprinted adhesive-backed address labels with your name and address and attach one to each child's name tag when you go on field trips. Add your phone number, too. The information will be helpful if a child gets separated from the group.

Bug Off

Carry a fly swatter in the car to use if a bee flies in the window. Take it along to the picnic table to shoo away flies and other insects.

Wash and Dry

Old cloth diapers make great drying rags when you wash your car.

Car Wash

Children love to help wash the car, so dress everyone in swimsuits and arm them with sponges and buckets. You'll all have a fun water activity, and your car will get clean.

 IMPORTANT SAFETY TIPS:

Remind children that soapy driveways can be slippery. Never leave children unsupervised around any water source.

Guideline

If storing items for child care makes your garage a tight squeeze for parking, make a guide to tell you how far to pull in. First, park your car in the garage exactly where you want it. Be sure support poles or storage shelves don't block car doors from opening and that you can easily close the garage door.

Next, hang a tennis ball from the garage ceiling so it touches the middle of your car's windshield. Drill a hole through the diameter of the ball and string a piece of clothesline rope through it. Tie a knot in one end of the rope at the bottom of the ball and use a screw-in hook to suspend the other end of the rope from the ceiling. From then on, whenever you pull into the garage, stop when the tennis ball touches your windshield. Your car will always be perfectly parked.

Perfectly Clear

Keep a new chalkboard eraser in your glove compartment to wipe off steamed-up windows.

Just for You

Read All About It

Subscribe to a magazine you really like. Take the current issue out to read while the children play in the garage. Read an article every day.

Your Own Ideas

Use this space to write your own garage storage and car trip ideas. To find out how to share your ideas, see appendix B.

_____

_____

_____

_____

_____

_____

_____

_____

_____

_____

_____

_____

Chapter 11

Yard:

A Place for All Seasons

New uses for wading pools, swing sets, and picnic tables create outdoor fun in your backyard, but don't forget dangers from sun, wind, and outdoor hazards, especially water sources. Hoses, buckets, wading pools, and all sources of water create potential drowning hazards. Always supervise children carefully when they play with water. Adding the ideas in this chapter to your creativity and safety awareness will help make your yard a year-round play space.

Outside In

In winter bring the outside in. Sprinkle wild bird seed and cracked corn in your window flower box to attract birds and squirrels. Children enjoy winter wildlife so close to home.

Bathtub Sled

Use an old plastic baby bathtub for a winter sled. Drill two holes in the front edge and attach a tow rope. Wax the bottom with liquid or paste car wax, and you have a baby sled to pull around the yard.

Snow To Go

Use your baby bathtub sled to haul snow for winter forts.

Spring Cleaning

Use liquid or paste car wax to wax your slide every spring. Your slide will last longer and be more fun to use.

Rain Drain

To prevent rainwater from collecting in your tire swing, drill several holes in the bottom of the tire. Rainwater will drain out.

It's a Breeze

Let the breeze entertain a baby while you play with older children. Tie a crepe paper streamer to a nearby bush at the baby's eye level, but out of reach. The slightest breeze will make the streamer flutter, and the baby will be fascinated.

Solar Heat

In late spring and early summer, watch the sun's path across your yard. Determine the sunniest spot and place your wading pool there first thing in the morning. By afternoon when you and the children go out to splash, the sun will have taken the chill off the water.

IMPORTANT SAFETY TIP:

Always disinfect a wading pool after use to prevent the spread of germs. Use a solution prepared in the ratio of 1 tablespoon of bleach to 1 quart of water. Pour the solution into a spray bottle. Spray the empty pool and let it air dry.

Water Slide

If your slide gets very hot in summer, tie your garden hose to the guard rail at the top and let water trickle down. Dress the children in swimsuits and watch them have fun on their water slide.

Foot Bath

To keep grass clippings out of the wading pool, make a foot bathtub to rinse feet before swimming. Put non-slip bathtub decals in the bottom of a square plastic dishpan. Fill it two-thirds full of water and set it at the pool's edge. While you supervise, have children step in and wash off the grass before entering the pool.

Time's Up

Bring your kitchen timer or travel alarm into the yard and set it for five minutes before the time to go in. The five-minute warning allows time to put away toys and helps prevent complaints when outdoor time is over.

Drinks To Go

Capped, individual-sized plastic juice bottles from convenience stores make great containers for children on the go. Save bottles and lids until you have enough for everyone. Write each child's name on a bottle using paint from a hobby store (nail polish works, too). Before you leave for the park or backyard, fill and recap the bottles. Store them in a cooler with drinking straws. The children can sip a cool drink and save the rest for later. Bring home the empties to wash and reuse.

Cooler To Go

Use a luggage cart or an old, heavy-duty stroller to wheel a cooler full of lunch to a picnic spot in the yard or park.

No Pushing

Prevent a pushed-out screen on your back-door by attaching a 4-inch wide flat curtain rod across the inside of the door at the height where children push on the screen.

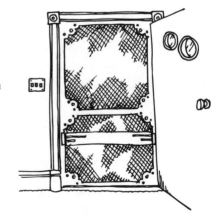

Tot Duster

If children are full of sand and dust, bring your mini-vacuum to the back door and clean them off. Get ready for giggles!

Ride Sharing

Sharing riding toys—and swing set equipment—can be a problem outdoors. Tie different colors of yarn to the toys or swings. Set the timer for turns. When it's time for the next group to have a turn, send them to the "green" trike or the "yellow" swing.

Taking Turns

Use Sweetheart Place Cards (see chapter 2) to draw names for taking turns on swings or riding toys.

Hit the Nail on the Head

An old tree stump in the backyard makes a great place to learn carpentry skills. While you supervise, let children take turns hammering large-headed nails into the stump.

Dome Home

A geodesic dome makes a wonderful shady summer playhouse when you cover it with a few old blankets or sheets. Secure with spring-type clothespins.

Catch This

Toddlers who can't yet catch a ball can still have fun with one. Cut 12 inches of nylon from the foot of an old pair of pantyhose and drop a soft ball into the toe. Tie the end of the nylon to the crossbar of the swing set so it hangs free. The toddler can push the ball away and catch it when it swings back.

 IMPORTANT SAFETY TIP:

Be sure the nylon is no longer than 12 inches to prevent a strangling accident.

Tent Maker

Use your swing set frame to make a giant tent. Sew or safety pin together two large, flat bedsheets along their short ends. With the sewn or pinned seam at the top, drape over the swing set. Wrap edges around support poles and secure with spring-type clothespins or diaper pins.

Tent Maker II

Use your clothesline instead of the swing set to make a giant tent. Drape flat bedsheets over the clothesline and secure the bottom edges of the sheets with bricks.

Picnic Table Hideout

Make a fun hideout by pulling out the benches of your picnic table about 2 feet. Throw a large sheet or blanket over the table so it hangs over the benches, too. Children will enjoy crawling in and out. This creates a shady spot in a sunny yard.

Sand Trap

Keep cats, rainwater, and leaves out of your sandbox with a plastic tarp. Anchor the tarp with sand-filled one-gallon milk jugs on each corner.

Cover-Ups

Protect the seats of riding toys from the elements by covering them with shower caps overnight.

Playpen Coasters

Keep playpen legs from sinking into the ground by setting them on plastic lids from coffee cans or margarine tubs.

Table Spread

Need a quick cover for your picnic table? Use a fitted twin-sized bed sheet—just the right size and it will stay put.

Construction Site

Use a plastic, hard-sided wading pool for a sandbox. Dig a hole in the ground the diameter and depth of the pool and insert the pool. Having the sandbox at ground level helps prevent tripping and keeps sides from tearing. If you care for children of mixed ages, consider making two sandboxes: one for the crash-every-thing toddlers and the other for the build-it-to-last preschoolers. Cover the sandboxes when not in use.

Carpet Cushions

Picnic benches are hard on little ones' knees. Use carpet squares to cushion the benches.

Magic Carpet

Brightly colored carpet squares make great seats in the grass for story time under a tree.

Safety First

Outdoor fun is ruined when someone gets hurt. Use these ideas to keep children safe when they play in the yard or park. These ideas help keep track of the children, prevent problems from sun and wind, and give you quick first aid for mini-emergencies.

In Full Swing

An often-used tire swing can quickly fray the rope it's hanging from. Use a length of old garden hose as a collar for the rope loop that goes over the tree limb.

Whistle Stop

Whenever you're outside, keep a whistle around your neck. Teach children to stop what they're doing when they hear the whistle. You'll have their full attention for announcements or emergencies.

Hold On

Bring your cordless phone outside during playtime so you don't have to leave children alone to answer the phone.

Create a holster for the phone. Sew a washcloth into a bag with a loop at the top. Put your belt through the loop and wear it when you go out.

No Tripping

Children can fall on jutting drain spouts. To prevent injury, wrap a pliable rubber sink mat around the spout's end and secure with nylon cord.

Ding Dong

Attach a large hanging bell to your backdoor so you'll always know when someone is going in or coming out.

Shade Maker

Babies sunburn easily. Use a rain or golf umbrella to provide additional shade over the infant seat.

Shady Safety

Place babies in infant seats under the picnic table. They'll be shaded from the hot sun and protected from flying balls and running preschoolers.

Wind-O-Meter

During windy seasons, fasten a pinwheel to a bush in the yard. You'll easily see from your window when children should wear their hats.

Bump Numb-er

Use a frozen juice pop to numb a bump on the mouth and distract an injured child.

Plastic Cast

When a child hurts a finger and you need a mini cast, use a small plastic hair curler. Tape will hold it on.

Cool Down

Children who are used to air conditioning get hot quickly outside. Don't let them get overheated. When you go out, give each child a cool down cloth, a thin washcloth that has been wrung out in cold water. Place the washcloths in clean rectangular wipes boxes and put an ice cube on top of each. Use a permanent marker to put each child's name on his box. Change washcloths each day.

Helping Hands

Outdoor activities with children can include jobs you usually do yourself. Children can help check an area before play, rake leaves, and clean up. Older children can help younger ones with coats and jackets, and you can teach all the children to pour their own drinks and do more for themselves.

Sticks and Stones

To prevent children from playing with sticks and stones, deputize some "Sticks and Stones Detectives." Decorate a large paper grocery bag with a crayon face. Staple the top shut. Cut a big hole for the mouth. When you first enter the yard (or a park setting), lay the bag on the ground mouth side up. Send the detectives looking for sticks and stones to deposit in the bag out of harm's way.

Bug Out

If bugs, leaves, or grass clippings get in your wading pool, give the children kitchen strainers or fish tank nets. While you supervise, they'll enjoy skimming out the pool.

Toy Wash

When yard toys need a bath, put warm, soapy water in your wading pool. While you supervise, give each child a sponge or old toothbrush and a toy to bathe.

Shooting Hoops

A large plastic trash can on wheels makes a great storage place for balls. When it's time to go in, have the children try to make a basket.

Backyard Gardeners

Let children plant seeds of their own in a special area of the yard. Mark each child's area with a wooden paint stirring stick, rounded side up. Push into the soft ground. Write children's names on the paint sticks with a permanent marker.

Backyard Gardeners II

Give each child a clean, empty plastic squeeze bottle (such as a used mustard or detergent bottle). Fill a dishpan with water, and let children fill their bottles using cups and funnels. Replace the caps. Now they can squeeze water onto outdoor plants without the flood a child with a garden hose can create.

Button Buddies

To get outside faster, use the buddy system to get coats and jackets on. Pair children who can button and zip with others who can't. The older children will feel important and everyone will have more time to play outside.

Zip It

Put a key ring through the hole in the zipper glide on jackets or jeans of small children who have a hard time with zippers.

Open Up

If the children can't reach the handle on your backdoor, it's easy to remove the handle, drill new holes, and reattach it so they can go in and out independently. Or, add a second handle at child level.

Patio Parking Lot

If you'd like the children to line up riding toys before going inside, make a patio parking lot. Use sidewalk chalk or masking tape to mark parking stalls and ask children to park their vehicles when it's time to go in.

Mechanics R Us

Silence squeaky riding toys with a squirt of oil. Play garage and let the children help. (Oil works on squeaky swing sets, too.)

Falling Leaves

When the yard needs to be raked, have the children help. Let them scoop arm-fuls of leaves and deposit them into the empty wading pool. Then let them help you drag the pool to the bagging or burning site.

 IMPORTANT SAFETY TIP:

Never burn leaves while children are present.

Falling Leaves II

Children enjoy raking leaves with small toy rakes, the type used in the sandbox.

Drink Up

Fill a push-spout picnic jug with ice water and place on a picnic table bench. Give children different colored cups and let them help themselves.

 IMPORTANT SAFETY TIP:

Don't serve sweet drinks outside. Bees may swarm around the jug and could sting a child.

Just for You

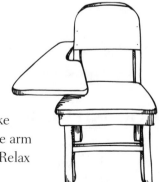

Have a Seat

Buy yourself a chair with an arm that folds down like desks used in school. Take it to the yard and use the arm to write a letter, do needlework, or rest your novel. Relax while the children play.

Your Own Ideas

Use this space to write your own outdoor safety and storage ideas. To find out how to share your ideas, see appendix B.

_____

_____

_____

_____

_____

_____

_____

_____

_____

_____

_____

_____

_____

_____

_____

_____

_____

_____

_____

_____

_____

_____

_____

_____

Chapter 12

The Room in Your Heart:

Labors of Love

You'll enjoy your role as a family child care provider more when you give more of yourself. Find ways to help your child care parents and do little extras throughout the year. You'll create a family atmosphere among adults who share love and responsibility for each child. Your child care parents will appreciate your personal attention.

Dotted Lines

Provide a clear parent-provider contract to be signed by you and the parents. Before accepting a child for care, sit down with the family and go over the contract line by line. Parents will have a chance to ask questions, and you'll avoid uncomfortable misunderstandings. Be sure all necessary forms are on file before a child starts care.

Picture This

When children are new to your care, ask their parents for a large picture of themselves that you can have laminated. When children miss their parents, bring out their picture.

Pinch Hitters

As a convenience to the child care parents, line up emergency backup care before it's needed. Ask a friend, neighbor, or relative if she would do an occasional day of child care in your home if you are ill or out of town. Be sure to follow your state's guidelines for substitute care and explain the process in your parent-provider contract.

Shhh!

Avoid telling parents about a baby's first step, first word, first tooth, etc. Leaving a baby in someone else's care is difficult enough for new parents without added regret from missing important firsts.

Bargain Hunters

Take the children on a walk to a neighborhood garage sale. Give each child a twenty-five cent allowance to shop with. The children will enjoy the field trip, and you just might find a bargain or two for yourself.

🛇 **IMPORTANT SAFETY TIP:**

Keep the quarters in your purse to avoid choking hazards from coins.

What's in a Name?

A mother may be disturbed if her child calls you "Mommy" in front of her. Explain that young children often associate feedings and diaper changes with mommies and that by the age of two, the child will have learned to call you by your given name.

Daily Report

Try to remember something special each child did during the day and share it with the parent at the end of the day.

Report Card

Create a daily report form you can give babies' parents. Include times the baby slept, foods and amounts eaten, diaper changes, activities, and comments. Make enough photocopies of the form for all babies in your care so parents feel they're participating in their child's day-to-day activities.

Winter Woes

In winter keep your walk and driveway free of snow and ice. If you have a neighbor with a snowblower, offer to trade a "Mom's Day Out" for a clear walk and driveway.

Tots' Togs

Provide bibs for every meal and snack. Parents often bring children to child care in nice clothing, so try to help the children keep their clothes clean.

Ready To Go

At the end of the day, be sure babies' diaper bags are packed and waiting near the door. Be sure the baby goes home in a clean diaper.

Ready To Go II

Make clean faces and combed hair part of your going-home routine. Parents will appreciate neat hair and shiny faces, especially if they plan to take the children somewhere after child care.

Accidents Will Happen

If your food program agency doesn't provide you with an accident report form, check with your licensing agency. Use carbon paper to make three copies so you can give one to the child's parents and send a copy to your licensing agency. File your copy in the child's medical folder. When you fill out the form, be sure to include the child's name, date of incident, a brief explanation of what happened, and the action you took.

Practice Makes Perfect

Conduct regular disaster drills for fire and weather emergencies so the children will know what to do should the need arise. Check your state's regulations about requirements for recording these drills.

Yearbook

When a child first comes to your care, take a photograph, record the child's height and weight, and trace a handprint on a piece of construction paper. Start a personal scrapbook or album with these items. During the year, add some of the child's drawings and write down cute stories about the child. At holiday time, give the book to the child's parents and start a new one for the next year. This will be their favorite gift!

Family Picnic

Hold an annual family picnic for your child care families. Invite parents and brothers and sisters and ask everyone to bring a dish to share. Get help with preparations from the children. Let them color special place mats, bake cookies for dessert, and pick flowers (or dandelions) for a centerpiece.

Money Matters

If asking for your fee on payday is difficult for you, put a pretty tin or decorated box on a kitchen counter or table near the door. Explain to parents that this is where they deposit their checks each week. Remove the container during the week, so parents know that when they see it, it's time to pay.

Treats To Go

When the children help you make a fun snack during the day, let them make an extra batch and cut into bite-sized pieces. Share them with parents at the end of the day.

Treats To Go II

Help the children bake cookies during the day. Let each child put one cookie for each family member on a paper plate. Cover with plastic wrap and send home at the end of the day.

Slumber Party

In early December, offer a Friday night overnight so the children's parents can do holiday shopping and wrapping without taking the children along. Set a fee and ask parents to sign up in advance. Order pizza and rent a videotape for evening entertainment. After breakfast Saturday morning, hold a cookie decorating party. Then serve lunch before the children go home.

A Cut Above

When you plan to take your own children for haircuts, ask your child care parents if they'd like you to include their children. Be sure to collect cash or checks made out to the salon or barbershop before you go.

Stone Soup

Choose a date for "Stone Soup Day" and have each child bring a different vegetable and a clean one-quart mayonnaise jar with lid. Read the story *Stone Soup* by Marcia Brown (Charles Scribner & Sons, 1975; this version of the popular tale is a Caldecott Honor book). Make vegetable soup with the children's help. Fill the jars and let children give them to their parents for their evening meal.

Say it With Flowers

In spring let each child plant a handful of quick-growing flower seeds. When the flowers bloom, let the children pick an "I Love You, Mommy and Daddy" bouquet to take home.

Top Secret Clearance

Keep confidential information about the children and their parents to yourself. Your child care families deserve your loyalty and trust, especially when they are going through tough times.

Check This Out

Start a child care lending library, complete with library cards, so children can take favorite stories home to read with Mom and Dad. Require that a book be returned before another one goes home.

Check This Out II

If any of your child care parents need help with child care or personal problems, avoid the urge to counsel them. Instead, offer to call the information desk at your library for books on the topic. Ask the librarian to hold the books at the desk so the parent can pick them up after work.

Birthday Surprise

Include a blank for parents' birthdays on your child care contract form. Mark your calendar, and help each child make a birthday card for each parent. You can trace the child's hand, have the child draw a special picture, or enclose a photograph of the child. Parents will appreciate the cards, and the children will be proud to give something they made themselves.

Celebrate!

Keep track of the children's birthdays and celebrate during the day with special menus and games the child chooses. The other children can sign a homemade card or draw pictures for the birthday child, or you can provide a small gift to make the day special.

Personal Conference

If you want to talk to a parent about a child's behavior or other concerns, avoid embarrassing the child or parent at pickup time. Instead, slip the parent a note asking for a telephone call in the evening after the child is in bed. Then you'll have privacy for your discussion.

Neat and Tidy

Once a month, or before a holiday or special party, treat yourself to a house-cleaning. Save a little money each payday. Then hire a reputable maid service to clean for you. If you have them clean on a Friday (while you take the children on a field trip), you and your family will enjoy a clean house all weekend.

Just for You

Gone Fishing

When you write your parent-provider contract, include a provision that gives you a week's paid vacation, three sick days, and two personal days off each year.

Your Own Ideas

Use this space to write your own ideas. To find out how to share your ideas, see appendix B.

_____

_____

_____

_____

_____

_____

_____

_____

_____

_____

_____

_____

_____

_____

_____

_____

_____

_____

Appendix A:
Free for the Asking

Materials for arts and crafts projects don't have to cost a lot of money. Many businesses throw away items you can use for child care activities. The businesses are often willing to give away or sell items at reduced prices. Put on your best smile and a cheerful attitude and ask! Here are some places to start:

Book, Magazine, and Newspaper Publishers

End rolls of newsprint and other paper are great for drawing and painting.

Carpet Stores

Ask for carpet remnants to use for sitting on during story time, to cover steps (secure to steps carefully), or to pad knees while gardening or sitting at a bench.

Cigar Stores

Sturdy cigar boxes with flip lids have many uses. Children love to keep their collections in these boxes, and you can use them to store crayons, markers, or office supplies. Get rid of the tobacco smell by grating a little bit of bar soap into the boxes and securing the box with a rubber band. After a few days, open up the box and discard the soap flakes.

Child Care Parents and Grandparents

Ask the children's parents and grandparents to save old greeting cards and wrapping paper. The children can use them for cut-and-paste projects.

Department Stores

These stores may throw out colorful foils and fabrics once used in window and case displays. If so, ask if you can have them for your art center.

Doctors' Offices

Ask for old magazines. Children can cut them up for collages and other projects.

Film Processors

The plastic containers from 35 mm film make great storage containers for beads, glitter, and tacks. Ask after holidays when the most film is processed.

Frame Shops

Heavyweight mat board is great for making game boards. Ask for the centers of the mats, which are usually discarded when a picture is framed.

Garage Sales

Watch for beaded purses, beaded curtains, and beaded car seat covers. Ask the garage sale holder if you can have them if they don't sell. If they know you'll use the beads for children to string, they may be happy to donate the items to your family child care.

Greeting Card Retailers

Unsold greeting cards go back to the manufacturer, but envelopes are often discarded. Ask if you might have them for preschool art. Let children use them for the handmade cards they make.

Grocery Stores

Ask the produce manager for the green plastic baskets berries come in. Also ask for the colorful plastic fruits and flowers they use for seasonal displays. If the manager is planning to throw them away, they may be yours for the asking.

Hardware/Lumber Stores

You may be able to get scrap wood for free or at low cost. Use the wood for creative building outdoors. Be sure to sand rough edges before giving to the children.

New Mothers

Baby food jars and cardboard formula cans are great for making learning games.

Printers

Odds and ends of paper in vivid colors make pretty scraps for collages, paper chains, and other projects.

Real Estate Agents

Each month agents discard computer lists, which are printed on only one side. The children can use the other side for drawing paper.

Schools

At year's end, teachers often have leftover art supplies they'll be happy to give you for your home art center.

Shoe Stores

Many shoe stores put shoes into plastic drawstring bags and discard the shoe boxes. Ask for the boxes to store toys or to make Valentine's Day mailboxes.

Tile Stores

Colored tile samples make fun game pieces for memory games.

Wallpaper Stores

Books of wallpaper samples can be cut apart for art projects.

Yarn/Needlework Shops

Talk to the owners about leftovers after their annual clearance sale. Yarn in odd lots, one-of-a-kind, and dated merchandise is good for weaving, bead stringing, and sewing on cards.

Appendix B:
Help Write the Book

Do you have an idea that makes family child care easier and more fun? We're looking for tips and helpful suggestions to add to future books. If you'd like to share your idea with other family child care providers, photocopy and fill in this form. Mail it to: Tina Koch, c/o Redleaf Press, 450 North Syndicate, Suite 5, St. Paul, MN 55104. If your tip is selected and you're the first person to send it in, we'll acknowledge your contribution in the book.

I have an idea that makes family child care easier and more fun and I'd like to share it with other family child care providers. Here's my idea:

_____

_____

_____

_____

_____

_____

You have my permission to use this idea.

(Your signature)_____

Name (Please print) _____

Address _____

City, State, Zip _____

Telephone number and area code (_____) _____

About the Authors

Tina Koch is a child care consultant and a teacher-trainer on staff at the Day Care Connection, a nonprofit child care referral service and CACFP sponsor in Lenexa, Kansas. She provides home training and workshops for the Day Care Connection and conducts training for other agencies across the country. While Tina raised her own three children, she spent more than a decade as a family child care provider. Her Certificate of Accreditation from the National Association for Family Child Care was among the "First One Hundred" in the nation. She has also served as a child care center director, preschool teacher, and Head Start aide. Tina teaches child care classes at Johnson County Community College. She continues to work for quality in child care and strives to make family child care a fulfilling career choice for providers and a loving home away from home for children in care.

Mary-Lane Kamberg is an award-winning professional writer in Olathe, Kansas. Her books include *Testing Program for the Developing Child* (Glencoe/Macmillan, 1994) and *From Patient to Payment* (Glencoe/Macmillan, 1993). Mary-Lane has written hundreds of articles about child care, parenting, health, education, and business. She teaches writing workshops for the Kansas City Writers Group and Johnson County Community College.